Bicycle Touring

Bicycle Touring

The Complete Book on Touring by Bike

Patricia Vance

Illustrated by Al Lassiter
Photographs by Michael Parente and Patricia Vance

Cycling Resources
books are published by
Van der Plas Publications, San Francisco

Publisher information
Van der Plas Publications
1282 7th Avenue
San Francisco, CA 94122, U.S.A.
vanderp@jps.net
http://www.vanderplas.net

Distributed or represented to the book trade by:
U.S.A.   Seven Hills Book Distributors, Cincinnati, OH
Canada: Hushion House Publishing, Toronto, ON
U.K.   Chris Lloyd Sales and Marketing Services, Poole, Dorset
Australia: Tower Books, Frenchs Forest, NSA

Cover Design
Kent Lytle, Lytle Design, Alameda, CA

Frontispiece photograph:
Montepulciano, Italy

Index by Kish Indexing, Rohnert Park, CA

Publisher's Cataloging in Publication Data
Vance, Patricia Jean, 1954–
Bicycle Touring: The complete manual on touring by bike
22.9 cm. Bibliography: p. Includes index
Bicycles and Bicycling, Handbooks, Manuals, etc.
Bicycle Touring, Handbooks, Manuals, etc.
I. Title
II. Authorship
Library of Congress Control Number 00-131376
ISBN 1-892495-27-9

This book is dedicated to Michael Parente, my partner in life and love. We have fun together.

Acknowledgments

Many people have helped me with this book. Some have provided information, opinions, and suggestions. Others have been sources of inspiration and encouragement. I needed all of you, and I am grateful for the support.

First of all, my tanks go to Michael Parente. This is your book as much as it is mine. I also want to thank Beth Boose, Dave and Katie Cushwa, Jeannette Bennicelli, Richard Dzjia, Donna Jackson-Kohlin, Ceil McColgan, Ellen Wert, The Art Nith gang, and many folks from the Bicycle Club of Philadelphia, including Harriet Herman, Ann Martha, and Joe Wilkinson.

Finally, I am grateful to editors from publishing houses that chose not to publish this book but offered praise, kind words, and encouragement: Alex Barnett, Darren Elder, Jill Hindle, Ann Kraybill, and Sally Reith. Your friendly and informative comments kept me going through several trying months. Thank you.

About the Author

Patricia Vance and her husband, Michael Parente, have been touring by bicycle for almost twenty years. Pat's first tour was a two-month solo trip through Ireland. Since then, she has traveled by bike as often as possible. In addition to bicycling, Pat and Michael sailed from their home in Philadelphia to Venezuela and back over the course of a year and a half. Pat is also a founder and organizer of "The Ladies' Hiking and Outdoor Society," an ad-hoc group of travelers who have been as far from Philadelphia as Italy and as close as Lancaster County, Pennsylvania. Since 1983, they have shared travel experiences as diverse as reaching the summit of New Hampshire's Mount Washington on New Year's Day and basking on the beaches of St. John, U.S. Virgin Island. At the tender age of 46, Pat sincerely hopes she still has many miles to go before hanging up her traveling shoes.

Table of Contents

Introduction

"Cyclotouring: Traveling by bicycle where the primary interest is sightseeing rather than speed. The cyclotourist makes frequent stops and usually carries packs. "
        Vélocio (pen name for Paul de Vivie), circa 1890

THIS book will teach you how to design bicycle tours that will take you wherever you want to go. It is not a list of destinations or routes. Bicycle Touring is a unique guide to choosing your own destinations and planning your own routes. There is information about picking a route, selecting equipment, preparing the bike, packing the bags, and getting everything there and back. It is also about having fun.

Why Travel by Bike?

A bicycle makes a wonderful vehicle for travel. Almost anyone can ride a bike, and it is fun. You can travel with ease far away from the crowd, or right along with it. It is fast enough to take you hundreds of miles in a couple of weeks, yet slow enough for you to relish the details along the way. You will make discoveries with every turn of the pedal.

As I cycled along the spine of mountains that rise in the middle of Puerto Rico, I discovered that bamboo has a voice. My husband and I paused on the road next to the slender giants soaring fifty feet above us, eight inches in diameter at their base. The stalks moaned and creaked as they swayed, sounding like a ghost ship rolling on its mooring. The wind whistled a low discordant melody as it found its way through the dense thickets. The woody leaves clattered like a baby's rattle rolled down the street by an inconsistent wind. We tilted our heads back to look at the sky; we were ants in the grass.

If we had been traveling by car or bus, we would have missed so much. The bamboo would have rushed silently past us at forty miles an hour, a flash of green as we hurtled toward the end of our journey.

Later, on that same tour, we rented a car to take us quickly to the opposite side of the island to meet friends. I thought it might be fun. The car ride would be just as enjoyable as biking, I figured, but we wouldn't have to pedal. I was very disappointed.

The scenery that had been so magical became just another forest. The unique jungle vegetation flew by so fast that it looked no different from the hills of our native Pennsylvania. We could no longer hear the melodic chirping of the coquis, Puerto Rico's tiny native tree frogs. My legs felt stiff, and I was restless after a couple of hours. I wanted to smell the pungent air and feel the breeze on my skin. We eagerly gave up the car and went back to our bikes when we reached our friends. There was so much to make up for.

The bicycle takes you out into the world. It puts you in a ringside seat. Sights, sounds, smells, and tastes come up to you, shake your hand and call you by name.

When we were in Italy, the wisteria was in bloom. Thousands of lavender blossoms tumbled down the walls of the houses and spilled over the pergolas. Its perfume was everywhere, drifting out beyond the town limits, beckoning travelers to come for a visit.

This heightened awareness is not limited to the landscape. Cyclotourists learn more about the culture and meet more people, both travelers and residents. Bicyclists need to stop at much shorter intervals, and they usually attract at least some attention. Whether it's New Jersey or Istanbul, people are interested in the bikes or the packs, or how far you have come, or what you think of their town.

We stopped at the side of the road just outside Assisi to fix a flat tire. A woman came out of the house and offered us lunch. Our Italian was restricted to asking for basic needs and getting limited directions, but we wanted to talk, and we persisted through hieroglyphics, a phrase book and sign language. We told her what we loved about Italy, and she told us how amazed she was that we traveled so far by bike and that we were welcome in her country.

On my first bicycle tour in Ireland, I had a great time but I learned a lot the hard way.

With public transportation, the schedules can interfere with your ability to decide when and where you want to go. Car rental is outright expensive in most places, and even buses and trains cannot compete economically with traveling by pedal power.

If you see something interesting as you bike, it is easy stop on the side of the road to investigate. Stopping a car at a moment's notice can be difficult. Is there a shoulder or a parking lot? Will you be blocking traffic? Is it safe? And you are not likely to persuade a bus driver to pause for a few minutes while you take a look.

As we pedaled from Santiago de Cuba, Michael glanced to his right and caught sight of a cave a couple of hundred feet away. To his surprise and delight, the cave had been painted with fanciful, mystical animal and human images. We stopped to explore, seeing more phantasms as we entered the cave. In a car, we would never have known those paintings existed.

A bicycling vacation also has the advantage of allowing you to eat as much ethnic cuisine as you like without fear that you won't fit into your clothes by the end of the trip!

My first cycling trip was a solo trek to Ireland. I had a wonderful time and I learned a lot about bicycle touring. I learned it the hard way, however. I discovered the flaws in my gear because something did not work when I needed it. I learned what I should have packed by wanting it when I did not have it. I carried too many items that I never touched. I realize now that I would have had an even better time if I had some coaching from someone with experience. This book is designed to be your coach. So turn the page and begin your journey to discover the world on a bike.

Part I

Route Planning

1.

What Kind of Tour Do You Want?

Choosing Your Destination

THE single most important factor for determining how much you will enjoy a vacation is how well that trip meets your expectations. If you have clearly defined what you want out of your tour, you are more likely to be satisfied. The more you know about your destination, the more you will appreciate it. The more involved you are in planning your trip, the less likely you are to be disappointed. Before you do anything else, define your goals and make sure you are taking the right trip.

Since you are reading this book, you have already made at least one decision: you want to tour by bicycle. However, there are many other choices you will need to make.

What Are Your Interests?

I like to learn something new when I travel. While beautiful scenery is a plus, it is usually not the most important factor in my choice of a destination. Places that are historically important or culturally different from my own rank high on my list of potential tours. I also do not balk at challenges. In fact, sometimes the challenge is one of the greatest appeals. The mountains of eastern Cuba are steep and the sun is hot.

Independent travel is rare, and so are hotels and restaurants. Cyclotourists need to be fully self-sufficient and comfortable with improvisation. But my tour of Cuba was worth double the difficulties that we encountered. While the Sierra Maestra mountains provide stunning vistas of unspoiled tropical rain forest, it is the warmth and generosity of the Cuban people that I remember most fondly. Despite poor skills in Spanish, Michael and I made friendships that we hope will last for many years.

But enough about me, what do you want to do on your vacation? Would my love of museums leave you bored stiff? Is an exquisite view more appealing? Is delicious local cuisine one of your favorite aspects of travel or will you be satisfied with a cup of Ramen noodles?

How adventurous are you? Will you be happy not knowing where you will sleep tonight or do you want the security of a hotel reservation? And what are your standards for overnight accommodations? Can you pitch a tent in a field or do you need a real bed every night?

Ask yourself, "What do I want to do?" not "What is the cheapest tour?" or "Where are the airfare bargains?" My family lives in Minneapolis. If I want to visit them but I see a great airfare to Chicago, I'm not going to buy a ticket to Chicago instead of Minneapolis. Price is always a consideration, and finding bargains makes the trip even more enjoyable, but you wouldn't visit your relatives in a city where they don't live, so don't spend your vacation in a place that doesn't interest you just because the price is right.

I have heard people say, "I don't care where I go. I just want to get away from it all." But for some, that means taking a mountain bike up a remote trail where they will not see another soul for weeks. Someone else might view "getting away" as ordering champagne from room service to enjoy in their private hot tub.

Think about enjoyable past vacations and figure out what made them fun. Be specific. Was it the company? The scenery? The excitement? Do the same with unpleasant trips. Were you bored or too busy? Was the weather terrible? Try to find common themes, positive and negative, and keep them in mind when you plan your tour.

To many of you, this is obvious, but I am amazed at the number of people who have not given a single thought to these questions.

Do it Your Way

Be sure that you are considering your own desires, and not those of your best friend or the tour organizer. They are not the same for everyone.

For example, Michael and I love Puerto Rico. The Puerto Ricans are friendly, the pace of life is peaceful and the scenery is wonderful. We recommend Puerto Rico to anyone looking for a warm winter vacation.

Michael's brother and sister-in-law, Joe and Barb, took our advice at least in part. So did our friends, Kathy and Pete. Both couples decided against going to the rural southwest, where Michael and I were. They bought package deals from a travel agent and went to the capital city of San Juan in the north east.

Joe and Barb had a great time. It was the best vacation they ever took. They came back golden brown, relaxed and rejuvenated.

In contrast, Pete and Kathy may have come back golden brown, but their trip was less than spectacular. People were constantly hounding them for money. The streets were dirty and noisy. The resorts were ringed with poor communities. And don't get them started about the traffic!

How can this be? Puerto Rico is a small island. How could three couples have such widely different experiences? Specific location was one difference. The mode of travel was another. An equally important factor was expectation.

Cycling in an urban environment can be confusing. Be prepared to change your route.

Michael and I went off the beaten tourist track and spent our time in the mountains and on the rural southwest coast. We traveled by sailboat or bicycle, both of which encourage a slow pace and more contact with local people. Joe and Barb, and Kathy and Pete stayed in the very big city of San Juan and its immediate environs. Cities are always very different from rural communities, no matter where you travel. In a city, you will encounter more noise, dirt, crowding, and poverty. Areas that cater to tourists attract beggars and others who want a piece of the tourist trade.

Of course, the city is also where you find night life, shopping, museums, a variety of restaurants and hotels and other tourist amenities. This is where individual taste enters the equation. Sun, dancing, and the slot machines were Joe and Barb's idea of a perfect vacation. Their hotel was right on the beach and it had a casino and disco on the ground floor. They didn't need to leave the building. All the noise and nuisance of the city didn't encroach on their vacation.

The perfect vacation for Pete and Kathy is something entirely different. They do not drink or gamble. They like to dance, but not in loud, smoky discos. They spent some time on the beach, but they also walked around the streets near their hotel during the day. This made them an easy mark for the tourist buzzards. They rented a car one day but never got past the "tourist limits." The car was expensive, the scenery was unappetizing, and the traffic was horrible. They would have been much happier in a small town on the southwest coast.

Package Deals

How did Pete and Kathy end up on the wrong vacation? They were lured into the spider web of the quick, easy, no-muss, no-fuss package deal. Package deals and other pre-planned vacations, including bicycle tours, sound great. Everything is taken care of by the tour organizer or agent. All you have to do is show up. Non-cycling packages including airfare and hotel are even cheaper than going on your own. Sounds perfect, right?

Sometimes they are. Joe and Barb were happy. But you should look carefully at what they offer versus what you want. You may find that one company will be better for you than another. It is also possible that you will be happiest planning your own tour, one that is custom-designed to suit you.

Deciding How Difficult Your Tour Will Be

Some tours are more physically challenging than others, and you should decide what level of difficulty you want. There are folks who are exhilarated by heart-stopping 50 mile per hour downhill runs and heart-pumping ascents that continue mile after mile. Others prefer a leisurely pace with frequent stops.

Several factors affect how much energy you must put into your bicycle tour. Longer distances obviously require more energy and time than shorter ones. The more hills you have to climb and the steeper and longer they are, the harder you will need to pedal.

Humans need to adapt to altitudes over 6,000 feet above sea level. Your body will have a harder time with the lower air pressure and decreased oxygen level. You will fatigue more easily and perceive a tour as more difficult. Even 4,000 feet above sea level can be a problem for people who are used to cycling at sea level. It is likely that you will want to travel at a slower pace and decrease your distance.

Unpleasant weather will also make a trip feel more difficult. Find out what temperatures are typical as well as the amount of precipitation you expect to encounter and be prepared for it. If the weather is hot, cold or rainy, the tour will feel harder. Again, your individual preference will be a factor. When we biked inland in northern California, the temperature was over 100 degrees for a week. Michael found it "a bit warm," while I felt like my brain was hard boiled. After we reached the coast, and the temperature dropped 40 degrees F, I felt like I had been released from a furnace. Michael bought a second jacket.

Cycling in cities is more tiring than in rural or unpopulated areas. There is more traffic and the roads can be confusing. This will slow you down and increase your stress level.

Going in Circles

We take a circle route as often as we can. You only need to make arrangements for transporting your bike to and from one location. We like to stay at the same hotel at the beginning and the end of our tour and leave our bike boxes there in the meantime. This gives us a convenient location to convert our bikes and gear from "airplane mode" to "touring mode" and back again.

Circle routes are easy to change during the tour. If you want to go a little slower, just make the loop smaller. Likewise, you can expand the circle to cover more ground. As you plan, note places where you can make your tour shorter or longer. Find roads that cut across or double back. Look for possible day trips. Think about places you might want to visit that are a little further away.

I buy our airline tickets before planning my final itinerary because sometimes it is necessary to wiggle my schedule around a bit. I may do this to get a better deal or because I cannot get a flight for my first choice of dates. In any case, it may affect the final schedule.

Rest Days

Put some days in your schedule when you do not plan to cycle. Free days can be filled easily on the road. You can spend a second day in a particularly interesting place, or just relax. You can always spend the time bicycling.

It is often easiest to explore and see the sights on a free day. It is possible to cycle a shorter distance and still have time to visit your place of interest in the same day. However, that can put pressure on you to arrive before your destination closes. Or you may find you are rushing your visit so you can arrive at your night's lodging before dark. Plus, you do not want to be too tired to see the sights when you get to them.

Days spent off the bike also prevent you from treating your tour as if it were a race. If you spend a day walking around town, or going to the zoo, it will remind you that your purpose is to enjoy your surroundings. It is very easy to focus on the cycling, to concentrate on how fast you are going or how many miles you have traveled. This is all part of the whole experience, of course, but there is little point in taking the expense and effort to get somewhere far from home and then rushing past, thinking only about your speed.

Also, if you run into situations that slow you down, free days will give you leeway.

Of course, there may be times when it is necessary to push on to the next stop as fast as you can. For example, the train schedule and the location of the nearest hotel makes it impossible to plan a leisurely morning ride. But overall, it is best to avoid stuffing too much into one day. Rather than focusing on how much you can put into your day, consider how much you can get out of it. Think quality instead of quantity.

The Importance of Being Flexible

Stuff happens. A road is closed. The weather changes. You get a cold and do not feel like biking as far as usual. You meet your soul mate and want to stick around and chat for a while.

You should have an itinerary before you go so you will not lose precious vacation time planning your route along the way. It will also make it easier to get back to the airport on time. At the same time, if you are inflexible, you may miss some wonderful experiences or force yourself to endure unpleasant circumstances. If you arrive with a plan but keep your mind open to better options, your trip will be more spontaneous and free-spirited.

It can be a balancing act to plan a tour. Sometimes you will need to sacrifice something you wanted to do in order to fit the rest of the trip together. Make a list, starting with the most important events or sights and continuing in descending priority. As you plan your tour, start at the top and work your way down.

Try to estimate how long activities will take. Add some additional time for unexpected delays, like standing in long lines. Then add on a little more in case your estimates are wrong.

When we were in Turkey, we camped about 55 miles outside of the ancient Roman city of Ephesus. We wanted to arrive the next day early enough to enjoy it before it closed at 5:00. By the time we broke camp at dawn, packed, and biked the 55 miles of hills and heat, it was 2:00. We were so hot and tired that we needed to sit down for quite a while before we had the energy to start walking. I remember very little about the scenery along that particular stretch of the Turkish coast except that it was hot. It would have been more enjoyable if I had planned to take my time getting to Ephesus, get a good night's sleep, and spend the next day exploring the ruins.

Ephesus was closed on the next day, however, so I had to make a choice. I had a few options. I could begin the tour earlier, and thus arrive in Ephesus a day earlier. I could have skipped Ephesus altogether. I could have stayed in Ephesus an extra day and shortened the route that followed.

Ephesus was one of the highlights of my trip to Turkey. In fact, it was one of the reasons why I wanted to go there in the first place. Skipping it was out of the question. Starting the tour earlier was difficult because of the availability of transportation from Istanbul. We considered staying in Ephesus an extra day if necessary, but we needed to bike the entire distance to the town of Bodrum by a specific time, so we would have been forced to bike at least two days with much longer than usual distances. Although it was definitely an intense and tiring day, I was still able to satisfy my craving for antiquities in a couple of hours. When we took off again the next day, I was happy with the compromise.

Reserving Lodgings Before You Go

Making reservations ahead of time will increase the pressure to reach a particular place at a particular time. It also decreases your willingness to change plans to suit your tastes. Most of the time, I prefer to carry a list of lodgings for the entire area of my tour and play it by ear as I arrive in each town.

If you feel you must make reservations, be conservative in your tour. Plan to cycle shorter distances than usual. This will give you a buffer if something unexpected comes up. You can also call ahead to your destination in the morning before you begin cycling. This gives you some security without boxing you in for tomorrow.

Another way to ease the worry of finding everything booked by the time you arrive is to travel during the low season or the shoulder season. Usually there are fewer travelers and the prices are lower. Keep in mind, though, there may be a good reason why one season is more popular than another. Sometimes the reason has nothing to do with the cyclotourist. For instance, summer is the high season in many places in the U.S. because children are out of school and it is easier for parents to plan trips. In some places, however, the weather or other factors may make it downright unpleasant in the low season. Also, you may find many tourist facilities, including hotels and restaurants closed.

Include non-cycling days to visit interesting local attractions, such as this one, Rosserk Abbey in Ireland.

Michael and I prefer to travel on the shoulder season, the month or so before and after high season. We find that prices are lower and crowds are smaller but most services are available. Even so, we feel more comfortable with reservations under some circumstances.

We almost always make reservations for the first and last nights of our tour. We usually stay in a hotel. If I know a particular location is very crowded when I plan to visit, I will make a reservation. For the Grand Canyon campground, which is booked six months in advance all year, I made a careful "best guess estimate of our arrival. Then I padded the estimate by reserving a campsite for that night and the one after. We arrived on schedule and we were able to use the extra day hiking along the rim.

Hotels usually allow cancellation of reservations without a penalty as long as you call 24 hours ahead. Most of the time it is very easy to estimate that far in advance. Camping reservations are not as easy to cancel without paying for them, but the fees are generally low, and the peace of mind they give you may outweigh the risk.

If you miss a reservation but are still charged for it, chalk it up as another trip expense and let it go. You are better off losing a little money and having a good time than pinching pennies and being unhappy.

For the record, I have never had to sleep on a bench in the train station because I could not find a room. Most urban areas have a telephone service to help you find a room. Also, consider hostels which are found in many locations around the world. A friend of mine has had success knocking on doors and asking if she could set her tent up on someone's lawn.

You don't have to drag your bike and gear around town. As they say, "Let your fingers do the walking." Find a phone, sit down, and start calling. Each place where you are turned down, ask for a suggestion of where to try next. It may require time and patience, but you'll find a place.

Camping Options

Being prepared for camping increases your options. There are more places to stop for the night. If you have an unexpected delay and cannot make your planned overnight accommodations, you can almost always find a place to put up the tent.

Carrying camping gear increases the weight of your packs, and you will have more "work" to do once your cycling day has ended. However, many of us don't consider camping a chore; we enjoy it. For some, a sleeping bag under a starry sky is the best bed in the world. Camping also offers the convenience of simply rolling the bike and gear onto the site. You eliminate the hassle with fitting everything into the hotel elevator, or carrying it up a couple of flights of stairs.

If you plan to do "freelance camping," that is, setting up camp in the middle of nowhere, you should allow extra time in your schedule to locate an acceptable site and get settled before dark.

I should note here that virtually all of the land in the world is claimed by somebody. Camping is allowed in most U.S. national forests as long as you are not visible from the road and do not deface or pollute the land. There are public lands in many other countries where freelance camping is acceptable, but in many places it is forbidden. If you camp on private land, find the owner and get permission. Some farmers do not mind if you camp on their land as long as you close the gate. It makes people mad if they have to chase their livestock down because you were careless. In any case, follow the rules, kids, and do not give them my name if you get hauled in by the authorities.

It is possible to combine indoor and outdoor accommodations. I usually camp about half to two-thirds of the time. We intersperse days in hotels as a change of pace and a bit of luxury. We also combine cooking and eating in restaurants. We don't always carry our stove, but we eat many meals on the road, especially lunches, and we eat dinner at the campsite as well.

In some areas there are no indoor overnight lodgings or places to buy food along the way. When you tour in these places, you must carry everything you need. Plan ahead. Be sure you have enough food and water to get you to the next town. However, in more developed areas, you may be able to find supplies and accommodations every ten miles. Tours to these places will not require as much equipment.

How much Do You Want to Spend?

Your budget will determine many of your choices. If money is no object, do you need a touring companion? ... I mean ... you will have more options.

If you have a limited budget, there are several choices that will be helpful. Camping is more economical than hotels. Buying food from grocery stores and cooking it yourself is cheaper than eating in restaurants.

If you hate to camp, hostels are a cheap alternative to hotels. Motels are less expensive than hotels. Still too expensive? Shorten your trip by a few days, choose a destination closer to home and drive or take a train instead of flying, or bring along a few friends to share the cost of the room.

The tighter your budget, the more research you should do. Careful planning will help avoid unexpected costs. Some additional expenses you may encounter include ground transportation (taxis, trains, ferries, etc.), postage/postcards/souvenirs, entry fees to events and attractions, renting a bike if you don't take your own, and buying the things you forgot to bring with you or break en route.

Take it With Humor

It is also very important to keep a sense of humor while traveling. If you keep a sunny perspective and take minor problems in stride, you will have more fun than if you let small irritations get the better of you.

Sometimes the most challenging and intense situations become the stories you tell over and over. One of my friends refers to these as "epics."

Our entire tour in Iceland was an epic. In Iceland's interior, there is nothing to stop the constant wind. We found ourselves hunkering down behind any rock that was as big as we were, or at least close. One night we camped in a gravel pit because it was the only place for miles that blocked enough of the wind to keep our stove lit and the tent from blowing away.

We crossed a river that was shallow, but swift and frigid. We took off our socks and shoes and plunged in barefoot. OK, it does not rank among the most "pleasurable" experiences of my life, but it was an epic. There is something exhilarating and invigorating about challenging situations. It leaves you feeling slightly holy and curiously fulfilled. And of course, it makes a great story to tell your friends back home.

Training for Your Tour

To get in shape, get on your bike and ride. No matter how great you are at some other sport, you need to cycle before you take a bike tour, although people in better shape will be able to start at longer distances. You will be sitting in the saddle, in the same position, using the same muscles every day on your trip. Make sure you are comfortable with that before you leave.

I took a hapless friend on a short tour. She did not bicycle very much but was an avid swimmer. So she is physically fit, right? Should be no problem, right? On the last day, her butt was so sore she had to put all of her clothes in a stuff sack and strap it to her saddle as a pillow. If we had spent some time cycling together before the tour, we would have discovered how uncomfortable her saddle was and would have taken care of it.

If you are a beginner at cycling, start riding five or ten miles. On flat ground, you should be able to ride five miles in under a half an hour and ten miles in under an hour, even if you are slow. When you can ride ten miles three or four times a week comfortably, you are ready to take a bike tour.

I consider this to be the minimum riding experience necessary for cyclotouring. You will be able to reach this level in a couple of months just by putting in the time on your bike. At this level, plan on riding 20 or 25 miles a day. Be sure you plan a route that is similar in terrain to what you are used to, that is, hills and climate of about the same intensity.

For even better training, I suggest that you take a few weekend trips, riding the same distance that you plan for your tour. Carry packs and try to make the terrain similar to the expected tour route. These will give you a feel for riding with packs and will also let you know how it feels to wake up after a long day and put another long day in. I think you will be pleasantly surprised at how well you do. In fact, if you take a couple of weekend trips, cycling 25 miles each day, you can pass "Go" and increase your expected touring mileage to 30 to 35 miles a day. It is as easy as that. I toured for years with daily averages of 30 to 40 miles and had a great time.

If you wish to take longer or harder tours, you will need to increase your training. It is very helpful to take a long ride every week or two. The distance of your long ride should be at least half your planned touring distance. Once you get to this level, you will be able to judge for yourself what your abilities are.

Even a beginner will be able to increase cycling distance rapidly. You can start the summer riding five miles a day and increase to 50 by autumn. The key is to get out and ride at least every other day.

When I decided to tour in Utah, I needed to increase both the distance and the difficulty of my training. There are no mountains in Philadelphia where I live, but there are lots of lovely hills. Michael planned a route that we nicknamed "Lucifer's Alley." It travels over some very steep hills, and some that are not very steep but continue for a long time. We tried to ride that route once a week.

"Lucifer's Alley" is only about 25 miles. I also tried to ride once a week on a route that was 40 or 50 miles long. This was about 80 percent of our planned average daily touring distance of 45 miles. That was more time-consuming and I could not always fit it into my schedule. However, I fit it in about three times a month. I rode over 100 miles a week that summer.

If you ride more than that, great! Take a longer tour. If you don't have time to put in this kind of mileage, no problem. Plan shorter tours. You will still have a great time.

Bike Clubs

Consider joining a biking club in your area. The Bicycle Club of Philadelphia has a large membership, and there are a dozen or more rides offered every weekend in the summer. One can find a ride at the right location and time that will suit any skill level. The club near you may not have the same number of rides, but it is much easier to find someone to ride with if you are a member of a club. I find that a scheduled ride with a group is a strong incentive to get out there and do it! Club members share information on biking skills, new routes and gear as well as providing pleasant company.

An additional advantage to cycling clubs is safety. People who ride with bike clubs experience an average of one accident per 10,000 miles of bike travel. The estimate for the general population is one accident per 2,000 miles. This is attributed to the increased knowledge of rules of the road and better skills in handling the bike.

People who do most of their cycling in clubs frequently have different attitudes toward biking than touring cyclists do. They tend to be more interested in speed and performance. They are usually fountains of information about bikes and gear. Both of these can be helpful to you. Just do not let them talk you into so many fancy techno-accessories that you do not have enough money left to take your tour!

It's Up To You

Choose the distance you want to cycle. Decide how you want to travel. Plan your own vacation based on your interests and ability. The more decisions you make and the more you care about what happens on your trip, the more fun you will have.

2.

Your Touring Companions

Choosing a Partner

A GOOD relationship between fellow travelers is essential to an enjoyable trip. You do not need to be best friends but you must

1.   be able to communicate amicably,

2.   be clear about your expectations, and

3.   understand and respect your companion's expectations.

Having a good sense of humor is never a disadvantage. Traveling of any kind can challenge a relationship. You may find you are spending a lot more time together than you are used to, in smaller spaces and unfamiliar situations. This can cause friction from time to time. However, the opportunity to become better friends and enjoy each other's company far outweighs any potential difficulties. It is also more fun to share your experiences with a fellow traveler. Mutual respect and an attitude of tolerance dispels most problems. Planning and discussion before the trip is also very important.

Before you go, you should talk about what each of you expects from the trip, even if you know each other very well. All of the issues we discuss in these first two chapters, and all of the decisions you make should be shared. If there are differences of opinion, it is better to work out a compromise ahead of time than to argue on the road.

If you want to push yourself and ride as fast as you can, but your partner wants to drift along, stopping at every new scene to take a photo, you will both be angry early in the trip. If you thought you and your partner would chat and get to know each other better as you rode, but your partner figures you will go at your own pace and meet up at the lunch stop, you are heading for trouble. Talk about it ahead of time and do not let your companions get away with, "Whatever you decide will be fine." Be specific and ask for specific feedback.

Dealing with Unequal Cycling Partners

It is more important to choose a partner whose company you enjoy than one who has similar biking skills. You will always have a better time with someone you like. But there are a few ways to keep you cycling together.

Michael and I try to level the playing field by handicapping Michael. He carries a larger share of the weight, slowing him down and putting us at about the same pace. We adjust the load as needed during the tour so that we are always working at the same level.

Bike club outings, like this one with the Philadelphia Bicycle Club, are good training and fun.

Some people believe that "fair" is everyone carrying an equal load. But true equity is when everyone arrives at their evening destination equally tired.

No one expects a child to carry a full pack, because children are not a strong as adults. The difference between two adults, especially a man and a woman, may not be as great but it is just as real. It is not easy to gauge equal output. This can be done using a heart rate monitor and training together ahead of time, but if you trust and respect each other, you can work it out.

Can You Handle a Fully Loaded Bicycle?

Michael and I redistribute the weight to bring us to the same pace for equal output. It is not because I cannot carry a full load. Anyone who has average cycling skills and strength can carry a full pack without difficulty. I have toured with people other than Michael. In some of those cases I was the stronger cyclist. Without my pack mule (Michael), I travel fewer miles per day at a slower pace. Do not opt for a supported tour group just because you think you cannot carry a pack. Plan to take it easy and you will be just fine.

Tandem Touring

Some people find that the perfect solution to the problem of unequal strength is a tandem bike, a "bicycle built for two." Usually, the stronger partner is the "captain" in the front while the less strong partner in back is the "stoker." It takes a bit of practice to work smoothly as a team, but once you get there, a tandem is a very efficient way to travel. It has been dubbed the "marriage counselor" by many happy couples.

Michael and I tried a tandem once and decided against trying it again. We rented one for a 60 mile ride. I am glad we tried renting first, because I did not enjoy it. I was uncomfortable without brakes, gear shifters or steering mechanism. The other disadvantage that I see is, well, not seeing. Cyclists on a tandem sit very close to each other and the stoker's vision is cut by the captain. You can see everything to your left and everything to your right, but nothing directly ahead of you. I am told that many people feel this way at first, but that it becomes natural after a while.

However, there are some stokers who never adapt. Husband and wife Joe Wilkinson and Harriet Herman met at cycling events and are both avid cyclists. They bought a tandem but after three or four times, Harriet said "no more." She felt nervous sitting in the back, not knowing when the next bump or swerve would come. Joe suggested that perhaps people who are already avid cyclists on their own have a harder time adjusting to the role of stoker. It is possible that a tandem works better for a couple in which one partner is a strong cyclist while the other is a beginner. This way they will grow together as the stoker's skills improve.

You might wonder why Joe and Harriet do not rotate the role of captain. Most tandems are built with the intention of putting the taller person in front. On the tandem Michael and I tried, we could not lower the front seat enough for me to pedal. A frame small enough for me as captain would be ridiculously small for Michael in the back.

In any case, for a tandem to work, there must be good communications between partners. The captain must be able to signal to the stoker ahead of time when there are any changes in speed, gears, direction etc. The stoker has to let the captain know how comfortable the ride is. The stoker must trust the captain and the captain must respect the stoker.

Unequal Partners

Some unequal partners like to travel with a larger group. Each person can find someone of about the same strength and skill and pair off. At the end of the day, the two can enjoy each other's company and swap stories.

If none of the above solutions works for you, one of you will have to slow down. The best way for two unequal partners to travel is by having the slower one set the pace by riding ahead of the other. Some people argue that putting the faster person in front allows the slower one to draft. By staying very close together, the first person will block much of the wind for the second person, making it easier to keep up. Racing cyclists use this technique, rotating the lead, to save energy. A group of cyclists all drafting off the one in front is called a pace line. But touring in a pace line is not very enjoyable. There is little reaction time for the second cyclist if the first changes speed or direction. The second person spends most of the time watching the first person's wheel. It is also more difficult for the person in front because one false move could cause an accident. With touring packs, it is tiring and unpleasant.

It is always a bad idea to push someone on a tour. At the very least, he or she will be tired and possibly annoyed. At worst, a person can become ill after prolonged overexertion. It will damage the stronger partner's vacation as well. If one person is in a bad mood it will create an unpleasant atmosphere for everyone else, especially if your partner is your significant other. You may find yourself sitting under a romantic moon drinking champagne by yourself, while your honey is already in bed, exhausted, angry or both.

Traveling With a Group

With the growing popularity of cyclotouring, the number of companies and organizations providing group tours has increased dramatically. Tours vary in size, difficulty, expense, and location.

I will admit right now that my preference is for independent travel. However, ultimately the way you like to travel should decide which way is best for you.

The biggest advantage of a group is companionship. You will see the same people every day for the length of the tour. You can get to know each other pretty well, and many folks continue to communicate with other tour members after the trip.

Organized tours may work out well for people who don't have a regular biking partner. We have already talked about them for partners of different strength.

Some tours provide a SAG (Supplies And Gear) wagon; a van or bus that follows the route and picks up anyone who does not want to continue. Also, groups usually have a mechanic to handle any problems with the bike. You can usually rent a bike if you don't want to bring your own.

If you decide to rent a bike, be sure that your tour operator guarantees that the bike will be fitted to you and is in good operating condition. The safest situation is to rent directly from the tour company.

How Much Time Do You Have for Trip Planning?

Taking an organized tour means you won't have to spend as much time planning your own route. (Of course, remember that letting someone else make all of your decisions is not a good idea.) The tour operator has also worked the bugs out of the route so you are not likely to encounter any unfortunate surprises. However, sometimes surprises are the best part of a tour.

The Constraints of a Large Group

If you decide to take a commercial tour, consider the size of the group as it will make a very big difference. The larger the group, the more orchestrated the tour must be in order to accommodate everyone.

You are on a schedule with a group. There is a suggested time to get started and usually a specific place for lunch. Recently I cycled with a very large group in Virginia. I would call it a road rally rather than a tour. There were 1,600 participants on a five day ride. The first campers were out of the tent by 5:00 A.M. It was impossible to sleep past 5:30. Half of the group was packed, fed, and on the road by 6:30. Three quarters were on the road by 7:00 A.M. Wake up at 7:30 and you may find yourself alone in an empty campground.

Since only one lunch stop is paid for, you'd better get there by the time you are hungry. You had also better get there before the food runs out. (Running out of food actually happened on the trip I took.) These are much less likely to be problems if you are traveling in a smaller group.

Of course, the crowd can be part of the attraction. Some of these road rallies are "cycling parties." The sheer abundance of humanity is the fun part. Anything else you encounter along the way is an extra benefit. It is all a matter of what suits you.

You can meet other travelers and share stories and information at campgrounds, such as this one in Reykjavik, Iceland.

Independent Travel

Commercial tours tend to lack spontaneity and adventure. They remove much of the risk, but when you eliminate risk, you frequently also eliminate the romance of travel. Being self-sufficient allows you to change your schedule, and to explore off-the-beaten-track places that you discover along the way.

We allowed ourselves the freedom to explore on our tour of Ireland and discovered some wonderful medieval sites. Ireland is full of ruins especially in the west where they dot the countryside. Most are undeveloped to the point of falling slowly into dust without intervention. Many of them are smack in the middle of cow pastures. Visitors simply jump the gate and wander around at their leisure. The sites are marked on the official tourist maps.

We tried to stop at as many of these as we could find. It was like exploring with Indiana Jones without the flaming arrows and rolling boulders. A tour organizer may plan a route that includes these sites. Frankly, it would be hard to find a route that didn't include at least some of them. But it so satisfying to discover them on your own and to be the only one there.

Also, my experience is that people traveling in a group are less likely to take the time to stop and explore, even when presented with the opportunity.

During my trip in Virginia, I was showering in the high school locker room used by those of us who camped. I heard one woman saying to another that the route passed some very interesting sites. The second woman agreed and said, "I want to come back here sometime and really look around. You just can't take the time to explore on a bike trip."

I was so surprised that I dropped my soap! That is exactly WHY I travel by bike. Admittedly, a group that large has an unusually strong "herd" feeling to it. But in all the group tours I have encountered and people I have questioned, there seems to be a push to get to the next rest stop and a sense of pride if they arrive at their evening destination ahead of the crowd. This does not encourage exploration or even pausing to relish the scenery.

Sometimes I change my plans because the tour is not working out as well as hoped. However, most of the time it is because we get advice from a local person or another traveler.

We were told about Fiesole as we rode the train into Florence. Fiesole is a small town that sits high on top of a hill just outside of Florence. The climb was our most difficult, but the view was worth it.

The town itself was quiet and provided a peaceful evening after a day of intense "touristing" in Florence.

Traveling alone or in a small group, you have easier access to local folks. Even the need to interact to find a room, get directions or order a meal involve you more closely with your environment. Traveling in a large group places a barrier between you and the area and the people. You lose some of the most memorable experiences of travel.

Local people are much less likely to approach you if you are in a group. On your own, you may receive offers of goodies and pleasant conversation that wouldn't be offered to a group. And you are less likely to strike up a conversation with someone who is not in your group.

Self-Guided Tours

There are companies that sell self-guided tours that provide a sort of middle ground between organized groups and independent travel. You are provided with a detailed cue sheet and map, and the hotel reservations are made for you. Usually, dinner and the next morning's breakfast are at or near the hotel. You carry your own bags and there is no SAG vehicle. While you will have fewer options and little or no flexibility in your itinerary, you will also have very little planning to do. Since you are on your own, you can set your own schedule and pace. The best part is that you will be more accessible to the local people and to other travelers you meet along the way. You will not deviate from the tourist path with these tours, but you will find yourself more intimately involved with your surroundings. They are also usually less expensive than group tours.

Helpful Hints for Travelers

As long as we are on the subject of hotel dining, I want to sneak in a quick suggestion. Hotel restaurants are almost always more expensive than other local eateries. Also, the food is often better and more authentically ethnic in other restaurants. Probably at least as important, however, is that you will meet more people at restaurants and cafes outside the hotel. And you are more likely to meet other people, locals as well as travelers, at less formal dining establishments.

Do You Want to Carry Your Own Packs?

I asked people who usually travel in a supported group if they would consider independent travel. I was surprised at how many said that they did not want the trouble of hauling full touring packs. It may sound like a hassle to carry your own packs, and I will admit that on rare occasions it can be. However, the rewards of traveling on your own far outweigh any inconvenience from carrying your own gear.

To say carrying packs is hard is not a very meaningful complaint. If we really wanted to do the easiest thing on our vacations, we would not be biking in the first place. Certainly driving a car is less physical work, and taking a bus tour is even less. In fact, if we really wanted a vacation that was not difficult at all, we would stay at home and turn on the television. Spend less money, sleep in a comfortable bed each night, communicate easily with the natives ..., but that would be a boring and unsatisfying holiday. So we accept that there will be a few events or situations that will be challenging. In fact, the challenges are frequently the best parts of the trip. Carrying full packs is a cheap price to pay for the joys of independent travel.

A Comparison of Touring Expenses

Organized tours are more expensive than independent travel. Non-profit groups, such as bike clubs, are closer to the cost of going on your own because usually no one is making a salary. However, if the tour is supported with a van or bus, you will be chipping in for that expense.

Your cost may be considerably more than the fee charged by the company. Find out exactly what is covered and what is not and try to get an estimate on your out-of-pocket expenses.

Commercial tours are much more expensive than independent travel. The person who planned your tour, the van driver, the mechanic and all the other support personnel have to make a living just like the rest of us and you are paying their salaries. This is fine, of course, however occasionally I hear someone say that commercial tours are as "cost-effective" as traveling on your own. Not true. I checked out a few of the most popular commercial tour companies and compared their prices to the amount I spent on a similar tour.

The price for a ten-day tour of Turkey with one group was $3,000 per person, excluding airfare. Michael and I went to Turkey for two weeks and then went to Greece for a week. Our total expenses, for both of us, for everything except airfare, was $3,000. Two of us traveled twice as long for the same amount. If you calculate the amount per person, per day, the cost of the commercial tour is four times our independent costs. This was one of the more expensive organizations, so I looked at tours of Italy with other organized groups.

The least expensive trip I found was $1,400 for one person for nine days, excluding airfare. If I subtract airfare from our expenses, Michael and I spent $2,500, or $1,250 per person. However, we were in Italy for three weeks rather than nine days.

That means we spent less than half as much per day than the cheapest commercial tour. You can plan your own tour and spend half as much money or stay twice as long.

Traveling with Children

Do not doubt for a moment the value of taking your children on a bike tour. Everyone I have talked to has had nothing but wonderful things to say about their experiences. The key to success is to include the kids in route planning and give them options. Listen to their suggestions and allow them to make some of the choices.

Beth Boose and Company

Beth Boose took her two daughters on two trips from Philadelphia to Hershey PA, about 200 miles. They chose Hershey because there is a large amusement park. As Beth said, "There was a reward for all that biking." The first year Beth went alone with Jalysa and Janiece, aged seven and ten at the time. The next year they were joined by her husband, Janiece's best friend Jenna, and Jenna's dad. Everyone rode their own bikes and carried their own panniers. Beth's husband pulled a cargo trailer. The kids rode what Beth described as "department store bikes," while the adults rode hybrids. Everyone wore a reflective orange safety vest and carried an emergency whistle.

The entourage made frequent stops, about every half hour or hour. They carried lots of snacks during the day, bought the food for the evening meal each day and camped most nights. The girls had no trouble traveling at least 30 miles a day. According to Beth, "You need to feed them all the time, but if you keep feeding them, they'll keep going."

Beth's group put the slowest rider in the front. She had the adults ride in between the kids, not allowing the line to get too far apart. She offers the excellent advice that the adults ride one or two feet to the right of the kids, putting the children farther from traffic. Children are sometimes not as stable or as confident as adults and a car passing too close can startle a kid more easily than an adult. Putting the adult a little more to the outside gives the child a wider space.

The Cushwa's

Big kids can also ride on tandems. When she was ten years old, Katie Cushwa of Barrington Illinois traveled over 1,000 miles as a stoker on a tandem. Her captain was her dad, Dave. Katie loved her trip from her home to Washington, D.C. and would love to do it again. Katie's brother David, then seven, took a two-day, 100-mile camping trip pedaling on a Trail-a-bike, an extension with wheel and saddle, hooked to his father's bicycle. The next year, Dave and David rode a tandem and Will took the rear spot on the Trail-a-bike. To make an even longer train, the whole family went on a camping trip. Mom Lynn and Katie rode single bikes and the boys added a cargo trailer to the back of the Trail-a-Bike! Dad Dave says, "We were all equalized…, to some extent."

Our trip to Italy was half the cost of the cheapest commercial tour. Here Michael enjoys the scenery in Volterra.

The Cushwas feel that this is a great experience for both parents and children. In his own words, I will let Dave tell you about his cross-country experiences with Katie:

> When we rode into a town, we would park our bike against the window of a little restaurant and go in to eat. People … would start talking to us. Next thing you know, everyone in the restaurant would be listening to us. [They told] Katie that she'll certainly never forget this summer and what a wonderful way to spend time together for a father and a daughter. We both really enjoyed the attention and inspiration. Katie would beam with pride and I would be welling up.

Reality Check

Not every minute of these two families' experiences were Hallmark moments. The Cushwa's underestimated how difficult the hills would be carrying all their gear. They were originally headed for Philadelphia and then Atlantic City. However, they found Pennsylvania simply too difficult to handle. So they turned south and took a much less hilly ride toward Washington, DC

According to Beth Boose, the first day of each trip was "a disaster." On one trip, they only rode seven miles before the end of the day. The bikes and packs needed to be adjusted and they experienced some uncommonly bad luck. A fall on the bike pulling the cargo trailer resulted in a badly bent rear wheel. The bike was not rideable so Beth and the kids went ahead to get help. Along the way lightning struck about 50 feet away, according to Beth's estimate, and nearly scared the life out of everyone. They were trying to get to a hostel and finally found a ride but there were many worried moments trying to link up with her husband. He got a ride from someone else and they spent much time going back and forth trying to connect.

Later, in the small town of Mount Joy, PA, some locals in a truck passed them shouting obscenities. The two dads told them they did not appreciate the use of such language in front of their daughters. A bit later, a police car pulled up next to them. The officers said that there had been reports of a "biker gang" in the area harassing local folk. Imagine how silly you would feel confronting three parents and three girls all wearing orange safety vests and carrying whistles, loaded with touring packs and pulling a trailer, and accusing them of being a "biker gang." When we asked if the police were laughing, Beth said, "Eventually."

Now before you allow this to convince you to stay home, Beth was laughing as she told us about all of this and everyone on the tour is eager to go at it again. First of all, it makes a good story. Second, these were isolated moments on an otherwise delightful trip. Beth and her younger daughter are looking forward to crossing the country together in a couple of years.

The Cushwa's are also looking forward to more trips. The hills were a problem, but not one that was unsolvable. Changing your plans mid-tour is not difficult. There is always a pleasant alternative to an unpleasant situation.

A Tour is a Journey, Not a Destination

Talking about her trip, Beth Boose told me that the most important thing to remember when traveling with kids is that the distance and the destination are not important; but having fun is. Change your route, shorten it, make it easier, travel fewer miles. Be patient. It's about enjoying the trip and each other.

Katie and Dave set up voice mail and handed out the number to all their friends and relatives at home as well as everyone they met along the way. Each night they would compose a new message telling about everything that happened that day and Katie recorded it. They also heard words of encouragement and congratulations that others had left for them. I can't imagine a better environment for building self-esteem.

Janiece, Jalysa, and Jenna had their own cameras and journals. At the end of each day, time was set aside for writing. Between the camera and the journal, they will have vivid memories of their trips for the rest of their lives.

Bicycle Options for Smaller Children

Jenna, Janiece, and Jalysa rode their own bikes. Katie rode on the back of a tandem. There are other options, especially for smaller children.

Pedal Attachments

If your child is too short to reach the pedals of a tandem, there are attachments that raise the crank and pedals. The pedals can be turned independently of the front rider so the passenger can pedal or rest. You can switch to the regular pedals as the child grows.

Tandem Extensions

You can get a removable attachment for a regular bike that converts it into a sort of specialized tandem. The Cushwas Trail-a-bike is one of these, and there are other manufacturers. They consist of a rear wheel, seat, handlebars, cranks and pedals on a frame that attaches to the back of the adult's bike. The kids can pedal at any speed and put as much pressure on the pedals as is comfortable. They can choose not to pedal as well. This gives small children the chance to help but allows them to quit and go along for the ride when they get tired or bored.

Dave Cushwa's only negative comment was that if the child leans out to one side too quickly, the bike can be pushed off course fairly easily in the direction of the lean. If the child is instructed not to move suddenly, the problem is solved. He recommends always keeping both hands firmly on the handlebars. He found that it requires more attention than a tandem or a trailer. But for children too small for a tandem, this can be an excellent way to introduce them to bicycling.

Bike Seats

It is also possible to attach a seat to the rack over the back wheel. This arrangement works for kids who are very young, toddlers. I have never seen a family touring with a child seat. I am told they make the bike fairly unstable because the weight of the child is so high above the wheel. Adding bike packs makes the whole thing even harder to handle.

Trailers

For very small kids and infants, pulling a trailer behind your bike works out better. There are some very good designs available. Check to see that the attachment to the bike is secure. Some trailers attach to the axle of the rear wheel, some to the seatpost, and some to the bike frame. Among the people I have asked, seatpost and frame attachments seem to be preferred. Trailers that have a swivel, allowing the bike and trailer more independent movement are given high marks. With these, you can lie the bike down while the trailer is still upright. In case of a fall, many think these trailers are safer. Not that lying the bike down is easy. Beth Boose has used a trailer with a swivel and said she would travel miles out of her way to find something to lean the bike and trailer against.

Cargo Trailers

Trailers are not only useful for pulling kids. They are gaining popularity for pulling gear. Most of the folks I have talked to would take trailers again, even if they had a few difficulties. The one caveat everyone seems to have is that it is very important that you do not overload them. Beth thinks this is why the rear wheel of her husband's bike was bent so badly. They are much more difficult to handle when they are overloaded, both because of the weight and because of the wind.

Some trailers have brakes. This may be helpful when you are going down a hill. If the trailer is very heavy, it can actually push the bike.

Mom and Dad's Job

All of these options allow children to work at their own level or to rest. However, they add to the adult's work and kids usually do not have much tolerance for sitting still hour after hour so plan to travel fewer miles. It is definitely advisable to try out your system (and your kids) with short weekend rides several times before you embark on a longer tour.

Other Passengers

We met two sisters who biked from Seattle to San Francisco pulling a hand-made fifty-five pound trailer carrying their eighty pound dog, Shiba. They were on a fund raiser for an animal shelter and Shiba was sort of a poster dog. Michelle pulled Shiba while Lianna hauled everything else. She had a trailer and front and rear bike packs.

Michelle found that the dog and trailer slowed them down considerably. They biked about two-thirds as far as they would on a bike loaded only with touring gear. Michelle also found that without trailer brakes, she was pushed down the hills. There was a good side of that. In the very rolling hills along the Pacific coast, Michelle was pushed fast enough down the hills that she had enough momentum to coast most of the way up the next hill, sort of a doggie- powered perpetual motion machine.

Surprisingly, Shiba was pretty content in the trailer all day. perhaps next year Michelle and Lianna will build a bike that Shiba can pedal and pull them up and down all those hills.

3.

Choosing a Guidebook

ONCE you have chosen a place that sounds like fun, you want to learn more about it. Where do you start? Go to the travel section of your local book store and zero in on your heart's desire. Most likely you will have several choices. Which one is right for you? It is possible that there will be several. I normally spend $50 or $60 dollars per tour. However, I have spent as much as $100 and as little as $17. That may seem like a lot of money for books and maps, but when you consider the cost as a portion of the total you will spend, it is not much. More importantly, the information you receive will make your trip immeasurably more enjoyable.

It may also seem like an extravagance in weight. I keep the weight down by using a razor blade to slice out only the sections I will need on the trip. I enjoy travel guides and often read the entire book cover to cover. It is like extending the trip. I also find that I enjoy my surroundings more when I am more familiar with them. However, the sections on history, culture, climate, and other general information will not be necessary on the trip. Also, as a cyclist you will travel to fewer sites than someone in a car, and most of the time the thick, heavy guidebooks cover many places than you will not be able to reach on your tour. So those sections can be left at home as well. I carry sections on accommodations and restaurants as well as specific information on groceries, public transit if necessary and other pertinent information. I carry the pages in a plastic sealable bag. When I return home, I take the sliced sections, place them back in the book and seal the whole thing with a rubber band. This way the book is still essentially intact and can be used again. You can also jot notes in a travel journal or photocopy the pages you think will be helpful.

Some books may seem at first glance to cover everything, but usually those books are lacking in some important specific information. It is best to consider the books that apply most specifically to your interests. Don't hesitate to ask for help if you don't see what you want. There are many ways to search for books by subject and they can be ordered if they are not in stock

Travel Books with Photographs

There are many books that are filled with lots of color photos and text that describe lovely sights and wonderful places to visit. They will give you a good general feel for the place and show you the most interesting sights. Often, they tell little or nothing about finding your way to and from the airport or which hotels are good and you will need to look at other sources of information.

Books with Bicycle Routes

There are dozens of books that give suggested bike routes for specific destinations. Some of these are written by organizations and some by individuals. Usually you will find these on the sports shelves, under bicycling although more of them are finding their way to the travel section. These are an excellent source of information. If you are lucky enough to find a book on cycling in your specific destination, I suggest you buy it.

Even if you change the suggested route rather extensively, as I frequently do, you can still learn much about terrain, climate, road conditions, and other specific cycling concerns that may not be in any other travel books.

In addition to book stores, route books can be found in bike shops and sports and recreation stores where bike gear is sold. Adventure Cycling (previously called Bikecentennial) has several cross-country routes, west/east and north/south. You can buy maps of sections of their tours. These give specific routes through any cities they pass.

These books provide a list of instructions to follow a specific route. Usually they also have a diagram or a map as well. The instructions are called cue sheets. Some books will describe geographic features, such as hills. Some will include the location of services along the way. Others, however, may give you mileage to the next turn and nothing else. I have included two examples of cue sheet in Tables 3-1 and 3-2.

Table 3-1: Example of Cue Sheet

Art Museum to Valley Green

about 10 miles, rolling hills

Distance (miles)	Direction	Road
4.2 (0)	R	Falls Bridge
4.3 (0.1)	R	Kelly Drive
4.4 (0.1)	L	Midvale Ave.
5.7 (1.3)	L	The Oak Road
5.9 (0.2)	R	School House Lane
6.1 (0.2)	L	Wissahickon Ave.
6.8 (0.7)	L	Walnut Lane
7.2 (0.4)	R	Park Line Ave.
7.4 (0.2)	BR	BC Hortter St.
7.5 (0.1)	L	Wissahickon Ave.
7.7 (0.2)	L	Wayne Ave.
8.2 (0.5)	R	Sedgewick Ave.
8.3 (0.1)	L	Sherman St.
8.7 (0.4)	BR	South Mt. Pleasant Rd
8.9 (0.2)	X	Allens Lane
9.4 (0.5)	X	Mermaid Lane
9.5 (0.1)	L	Woolcott Road
9.8 (0.3)	R	Valley Green Lane
10.4 (0.6)	L	Valley Green Restaurant

Legend

R	Right
L	Left
QR	Quick Right
QL	Quick Left
BR	Bear Right
BL	Bear Left
X	Cross
BC	Becomes
TSO	To Stay On

Do not limit yourself to the routes suggested in the book. It is not the only acceptable route, or even necessarily the best for you. It may have been so for the author, but you most likely will have different tastes, expectations, and skills. Consider the advice and information provided and use the suggested route as a starting point. You can at least be sure the roads suggested are acceptable for cycling, but allow yourself the freedom to add or subtract locations, change the daily distances, and generally stray when some other plan would suit you better.

Sometimes a particular route becomes very popular and you will meet others following the same plan. Route 1 on the U.S. west coast is

---

Table 3-2: Example of Cue Sheet
Lazy Creek Loop

35 miles, Hilly

0.0 (0.0)	Leave the parking lot at Lazy Creek Campground and turn right on Creek Road. Lazy Creek has overnight camping and a camp store. There is a café a mile away on Highway 1.
1.8 (1.8)	Junction with State Road 4005; turn left
4.5 (2.7)	Y, bear right to stay on SR 4005.The route becomes hilly here with a long climb after the town of Bridgeport.
7.8 (3.3)	Intersection in Huntington. Turn left on Elm Street. There is a grocery store on Maple Lane, two blocks on the right.
9.4 (1.6)	Intersection. Turn right on College Road.
9.8 (0.4)	College Road becomes highway 12. There are many hills along this road, however, they are short and none are very steep
12.6 (2.8)	Junction with Township Line Road. Turn left.
18.3 (5.7)	Intersection in Bailyville; Township Line Road becomes Main St. Sandy's Café on Main St.
23.1 (4.8)	Y, bear right to stay on Township Line Road.
26.9 (3.8)	Junction with Creek Road. Turn left. This section of Creek Road is rolling for about 4 miles, then it is flat to the campground parking lot.
35.0 (8.1)	Lazy Creek Campground parking lot.

---

one example. *Bicycling the Pacific Coast* by Kirkendall and Spring is a popular book that entices many people to try this route. When we followed part of the route starting about 300 miles north of San Francisco, we met many interesting and enjoyable folks and had pleasant experiences sharing stories and goodwill. We met the ladies with the dog trailer, a German couple riding the entire length of California, and an existential philosopher, sort of a Jack Kerouac on a bicycle.

I know cyclists who travel with only a route book and no other books or maps. I do not recommend it. The problem is that they know nothing about the area just off the route. They are unable to alter the route for any reason. I doubt that the authors intend these to be your only source of information. Besides, every book, including the one you are now reading, is going to be wrong at least once. You can not expect an author to be able to keep up with every detail of the route year after year. Most books are not updated every year anyway. OK, so they probably didn't flatten the colossal hill described, but that quaint little B&B may be an auto body shop today. Mistakes in mileage are very easy to make and probably every route book contains at least one. If you have a map in addition to the suggested route, you can catch mileage errors. If you have information about the area surrounding the route, you will be able to compensate when the route is not exactly as expected.

We could take bikes on the trains in Italy, but only if they were packed to be carried by hand.

Traditional Guide Books

Cycling route books are almost always short on information on places to sleep and eat, as well as sightseeing. For this you will need more traditional travel guide books. Go back to the travel section. Scan the titles and be as specific as you can. There will be a zillion books on France, but only a couple about Brittany, for instance. You may need to go back to the ones on France, but see what you can do with the more local and specific ones first.

The number of travel guide books seems to grow every time I go to a book store. You can easily find a dozen books on the most popular travel destinations and you may even find more than one to the most remote spot you can think of. Choosing one that is right for you may seem daunting. I have listed questions that you can ask yourself as you browse. These will help you zero in on a book or two that is written for the vacation you want to take.

1.   Overall tone and style

Is the writing style formal or casual? Does the author express a sense of humor? Does the author seem fussier than you? Does it sound as though you will be roughing it more than you would like? Does the author stress comfort and luxury or is economy the bigger focus?

2.   What lodgings and restaurants are listed?

This will tell you a lot right off the bat. Are the kinds of accommodations you want listed? Are you camping or staying indoors? Are you staying in hotels, motels, B&B's, hostels? Do the descriptions sound good to you? Are the listings within your price range? Many guide books cater to a particular group. You want to be sure they are catering to *your* group.

Take a look at the restaurant listings also. Are they in the right price range and sound like someplace you would like to go?

Remember that once a location is listed in a guidebook, especially a popular one, the price may go up and it may be more crowded than described. In any case, quality can change rapidly, whether you read about it in a book, heard about it from a friend or were there yourself five years ago.

3.   Does the author recommend things to do and see?

Some books cover only the most common tourist stops. Some cover only the most exotic and remote locations. Most books will have a little of each but will lean more or less heavily in one direction. Do you want to visit places off the beaten track? Do you want to avoid the tourist spots altogether? Check to see if there is a list of "best sights" or something similar. Do these seem like the kinds of places you would like to visit? If they do, the rest of the book is more likely to fit into your plans as well.

4. Are other travelers services described?

You will need to know the location of specific services, such as bike shops and laundries. If you are cooking your own food, you will need to know which towns along the way have grocery stores. Are these listed anywhere? They probably will not be with restaurants. Try looking under the descriptions of individual towns. You may need to transport yourself and your bike by public transportation. Is there any information about primary lines or schedules?

Are banks listed? What about places to change money? How difficult is it to change money? What are the normal business hours and what days of the week are they usually open? Some of these will be listed in the front of the book under "general information" or something similar. They may also be listed under descriptions for individual towns.

5. What about hours and days of opening and admission charges for museums and other attractions?

Along with a description of the attraction, there should be practical information to help you plan your itinerary.

6. Are special events listed by date for the entire year?

If a holiday is listed, does the author tell you about hotel room availability? Some special events are attended only by locals and rooms are not a problem. However, if you are biking into New Orleans during Mardi Gras, you had better have reservations. A good description of celebrations can help you decide if you want to participate or start biking in the opposite direction.

7. Are only the largest towns described?

Can you tell from the descriptions if a town is just a dot on the map or if there will be tourist services available? As a cyclist, you need more of this information than a motorist who can drive in an hour or two a distance that will take you all day. Does the book give details on only the biggest towns and tourist spots? If so, try to find something more detailed.

8. Does the book include suggested itineraries?

Suggested itineraries in non-cycling books are usually aimed at motorists. A biker on vacation usually cannot complete these in a couple of weeks. However, you may be able to complete a two or three day car trip in a week or two. You may also learn about some good roads with lovely views or attractions. Most suggested walking tours can be biked. Although, of course, you can always tether your steed and be a pedestrian for a day.

9. Is there anything about bicycling?

With all books that are not specifically about cycling, turn to the index and look up "cycling" or "bicycling." Check the pages listed to see how in tune to cycling the guidebook will be. The mere mention of bicycles gives a little insight. A book that talks about bike touring at all is likely to be written for the independent traveler (that's you!). The more information, the better for you, but don't discount a guidebook because it does not recommend cycling. You can still learn from them, just adapt their advice to your needs.

When I read a guidebook on Iceland, there was a brief section on biking. Basically, it was a litany of why one would not want to tour in Iceland by bike even though a few crazy folk do. The author listed the relentless wind, unpaved roads, and cold weather. She described cyclists as either masochists or ignorant of the conditions they would encounter.

When I read this passage, I did not give up my plans, but I did take the reasons the author gave into consideration: I rode a mountain bike, brought wool clothing, and planned low daily mileage.

10. What if there is no mention of cycling?

Whether you are reading about cycling or not, there are ways to gather as much relevant information as possible. Look for descriptions of the climate, including temperature and precipitation. Any good travel guide should at least provide monthly averages for these, as this is important to all travelers.

There may also be descriptions of the amount of sunshine or cloud cover. Do they say anything about the wind? It is nice to know the direction of the prevailing wind so you can put it to your back, or at least be prepared for a head wind and plan accordingly. Check for descriptions of the local vegetation. Phrases like "low plant life" and "twisted, stunted trees" are a give-away to wind or cold or both.

11.   Is there any description of driving conditions?

Most guidebooks will tell about driving conditions. You will probably be biking on roads most of the time, so any information will be useful. What are the road conditions? Good repair or neglected? Heavy traffic? Isolated streets? Polite or aggressive drivers?

Pay attention when the author writes "after a long climb, you will burst upon a breathtaking view of the valley where you came from, far, far below." That is going to be a long hard up hill ride. In fact, many "scenic vistas" are located at the tops of hills as you usually need to be high above the land you are looking at in order to take it all in.

12.   Will you need to communicate in a foreign language?

If you are going to a country where you do not speak the native language, see if you can get a book with some information. Is there a short dictionary and a pronunciation guide? Is there a list of common phrases? Are they phrases you think you will use? You should learn the words for "Thank you" and "Hello" but you probably will not need to say "Please have the bellhop carry my bags to the limousine" or "Not too much starch in my shirts, please."

It is always a good idea to carry a pocket dictionary and a phrase book whenever you are not fluent in the local language.

13.   Is there an introduction to local customs?

For cultures that are quite different from your own, it is very helpful to have a section on customs and manners so that you will have some idea of what behavior is polite. It is easy to make a mistake in this area, however, most of the time people will not be insulted. In most countries people accept that others have different mores and accept that you meant no offense.

14.   Are there sketch maps showing streets in major towns?

It is nice to have city and town maps in a guidebook. For biking you will need better quality maps to navigate from town to town,

Table 3-3: Evaluation of travel book series

Series name	IT	Prices	P	SI	Itin	Glos	*
Access		M					
Berlitz			X			X	
Blue Guides	X	L, M, E			W		X
Cadogan	X	L, M		X		X	X
Essential		L, M	X			X	
Eyewitness		L		X			X
Fodor		L, M				X	
Frommer		L, M					
Insight		L, M	X				
Lonely Planet	X	L, M, E, C					X
Let's Go	X	L, M, E, C				X	X
Michelin		I	X			X	
Michelin in Your Pocket			X		W, D	X	
Rick Seve		I			W, D	X	
Rough Guide	X	L, M, E, C	X			X	X
Thomas Cook					W, D	X	

Legend:

IT: Independent traveler. Enough basic information to plan and arrange your own trip.

Prices: L = Luxury; M = Moderate; E = Economy; C = Camping

P: Good photographs

SI: Special interest books

Itin: Suggested itineraries: W = Walking; D = Driving tours

Glos: Foreign language glossary and/or phrases

*:   The author has used this series and liked it.

but sketch maps of the route and street maps of towns along the way are helpful.

Other Books

You may be interested in books that are not about general traveler's information. There are books devoted to a particular place covering cuisine, history, literature, native plants and animals, fishing, religion, art, golf, and on and on. If you have an interest that you would like to incorporate into your tour, ask a librarian or book store employee to help you search for a book about it.

Travel Book Publishers

There are many guide book series. Sometimes one author writes every book in the series and sometimes the author changes with each book. Even when the author is the same, the quality of different books in a series can vary dramatically. However, there is usually a tone and quality that is the standard for each. With that in mind, Table 3-3 provides you with my opinions about some of the series of travel books.

I used a code system to categorize each series and help you decide if a series is aimed at you.

My favorite guides are those published by Lonely Planet. However, I also use Blue Guides, Rough Guides, and Let's Go. Cadogan and Eyewitness are not usually nuts-and-bolts kind of guides, but they are great for particular niches of travel. Rick Steve's has driving tours that can be adapted to biking, albeit with shorter daily distances.

The Mountaineers and Countryman publish many books that include bike routes. Some of these are for extended tours, while others are for only one day. However, there are usually a few single day tours that are close together. You can easily patch these together for a longer trip.

I also want to mention the Culture Shock series of books. These are extensive sources of information for culture, customs, and etiquette. These features make them most helpful for those who plan to spend an extended time in another country.

4.

Selecting a Route

WHEN you have figured out where you want to go and what you want to see, it is time to start mapping your route.

A road map is a great place to start. You can buy one from a book store or get one free from the tourism office for your destination. Use your road map to outline your route before looking at more detailed maps such as topographic maps or bike routes.

Road maps are designed for use by motorists, but they also provide useful information for bicyclists. Usually, motorists don't care about the details along any given road, as long as it's going where they want it to. However, for cycling, the location of bridges, tunnels, railroads, intermediate towns, parks, and other facilities is very helpful.

A Rough Outline of Your Route

Use the map's scale of miles to quickly estimate about how far you can travel. Multiply your daily distance by the number of days you will be cycling. Keep in mind that you may want to have a few non-cycling days for sightseeing. Plan a tentative loop around the area of your tour including as many of your chosen sights as possible. Don't take the time to plot accurate mileage the first time around. Your quick estimate will be shorter than the actual mileage because of turns in the road and other features that you will not consider here. If you plan that this projected mileage is about fifteen percent lower than the true mileage, you will have a reasonable estimate. Consider several tentative routes if possible.

Most road maps have points of interest marked. Maps from tourism offices are especially good about this. You will find scenic vistas, historic sites, parks, public beaches, botanical gardens, and many other places that you should consider visiting. Even if you know little or nothing about something listed, consider stopping just for the heck of it. Allow yourself to be surprised. It may turn out to be boring, a tourist trap or inaccessible, or it may be a gem. Be adventurous at least a couple of times along the way. The search itself is fun and rewarding enough to justify the exploration.

If the places you want to see are located far apart, consider taking a train, ferry, or bus between long sections.

Once you have a general idea of your tour direction and distance, you can refine the route.

Measuring Distance

Most road maps have at least some distances marked. The small roads that are optimal for bike touring may not be marked and you will need to determine the mileage yourself.

There are a number of devices designed to measure distances on maps. I use a simple mechanical device. The one I use (Figure 4.1) has a small wheel that I roll along the map. This turns a dial that moves along a scale much like hands on the face of a clock.

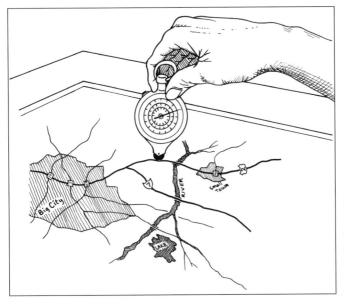

Fig. 4.1.
Use of distance measuring wheel to determine the length of the route.

First, I run the wheel over the map's scale of miles and note how many tick marks the dial passes for each mile. Then I count the number of tick marks the dial passes as I roll the wheel along my route and I convert the ticks to miles. This method is very accurate. I bought my distance measuring wheel from a store that sells boating supplies. They are also available from stores that specialize in travel gear or maps.

I also found that a handmade scale of miles works very well, although it is not as accurate as the wheel. It is, however, always available. Take a small piece of paper or a string and mark miles on it with a pen, using the map's scale of miles in the map legend. Place your scale along the route to measure distances.

The distances given on the map can be considered correct. However, no matter how careful you are, it is hard to get an accurate reading from a road map.

There are slight turns in the road that the map cannot show because of the scale. These turns are counted by the map maker, but you may not have enough detail to be as accurate. For road maps and other small-scale maps, you will need to add five or ten percent to your estimate.

You will be measuring only the flat distance and not any addition due to hills, both up and down. Therefore, in hilly terrain, increase your estimate by two or three percent.

Areas that show switchbacks will be difficult to accurately determine and another two or three percent should be added to areas where they appear. This means that if you are measuring a road map in a hilly area with switchbacks, you should add 10–15 percent to your final calculation.

When you switch to larger scale maps, your estimates will be more accurate and it will only be necessary to add a few percent to account for the rise and fall of the road in hilly locations. If you know your geometry, you can calculate this very accurately. I just add a little bit to my estimates and accept that my measurements will not be perfect.

Even with large-scale maps, a road that makes many turns and switchbacks may be impossible to measure accurately due to the lack of detail. It is better to overestimate mileage than underestimate it. If you are in doubt, increase your estimate.

I begin to keep a notebook at this point, writing the distances between all significant points along my potential route. This includes towns, places of interest, parks, campgrounds and areas that might have groceries or restaurants. Some of these may become overnight stops or possibly lunch or grocery stops. As I fine-tune the route, having as much information as possible will help me make my decisions. It is helpful to check with your guidebook as you go.

Which Roads Are Best?

The best roads will be scenic, interesting, in good repair, have little car traffic, and pass through enough towns that you will be able to get the services you need. You won't have the luxury of checking the roads out by car ahead of time if you are traveling far from home. However, your educated guesses work out just fine in most cases.

Scenic roads are marked on road maps and are a good place to start. Some are narrow and must handle many cars, however, so don't assume they will be quiet shady lanes. Try to get information ahead of time. The local department of transportation or tourism office will be able to help. Try the Yellow Pages to get a phone number. Your local library will have Yellow Pages for most cities. You may also be able to contact them through the Internet if they have a Web page. If you search for the name of your destination and "tourism" or "transportation," you should be able to find it.

You should eliminate the limited access highways right away. You wouldn't be safe or welcome; you might even find yourself facing a stiff fine.

Look for major roads that have smaller roads running in approximately the same direction. Cars will almost always go for the major route where they assume they can go faster. You'll be happier on the smaller route. Most roads that parallel interstates will be good bets for this reason. In towns and cities, they may be lined with commercial buildings, not the best view. This is not likely to be the situation in rural areas.

County and state roads are usually better for bike travel than federal (interstate) roads. The federal roads tend to be larger and to go directly from one populated area to another, which makes them attractive to motorists.

Secondary roads that are the only or the primary link between populated areas are frequently bad choices. They are likely to have more traffic and to be too small to handle it. Smaller roads are less likely to have shoulders than larger roads. A road with a lot of traffic but no shoulder will make very unpleasant biking. Try to find routes that are smaller and less direct than another nearby road. You may travel over more miles to arrive at the same destination, but you will be happier.

Even the most direct route through largely unpopulated areas will probably have little traffic.

Small roads tend to be narrow and to have buildings and trees right next to the road edge. This is an advantage in a head wind or on hot days, as they will cut the wind and provide more shade than a wide open highway.

Avoid places where many roads funnel together. These will have more traffic and may be confusing.

Sometimes, there is no really good option for a particular section of the tour. When this is the case, you may want to make a major change in your tour. On the other hand, you may decide to grit your teeth and get through it as quickly as you can. If you must travel on a major roadway, think about when there will be the least amount of traffic. For example, try to avoid traveling during rush hour. perhaps you want to rise a little earlier or a little later that day and hit the road when everyone else is in bed or at work. Or try scheduling that leg on a weekend.

If there are no towns for miles along one leg, you will have to carry extra food and water.

If you run into too many problems along a route, start over. Head a different direction this time. It is not possible to come up with the perfect route for every leg of every tour. Just take a deep breath and remind yourself that you will be on a more pleasant road soon.

Hills

Plan lower mileage for days with many or steep hills. Give yourself time to rest more often or even to walk part of it if you need to. Hilly roads also usually afford more opportunities for wonderful scenic overlooks. You will want to stop and admire them.

The best source of information on hills is a topographic map. However, road maps are also valuable.

A road with a steep grade is a potential problem for trucks. Because of this, grades of five percent or more are frequently marked with an arrow pointing up the direction of the incline. Even if primary roads are marked, it is possible that smaller roads, not suitable for trucks, will not be. If you see an arrow on a highway near your route of choice, you can bet your road will be hilly, too. Primary roads are usually less hilly than secondary ones.

Many maps show some topography by using different colors. Usually, the low areas are green and gradually fade to brown and tan, but check the legend. In any case, many colors in one area means you will encounter hills.

The presence of switchbacks is a dead giveaway to a very steep hill. Look for names like "Mountain View," "Hillsboro," "Mt. Fuji," etc.

Cyclists usually talk about percent grades. If a road rises 100 feet over a distance of 1,000 feet, that is a 10 percent grade. Number of degrees is another common method of measuring grade. The same 10 percent grade road is 4.5 degrees. You can see why it makes a better story to use percentage; it sounds about twice as steep.

But what does *that* mean? Cars have difficulty climbing anything over 15 to 18 percent. So the steepest road you have ever seen is probably about 18 percent.

An 8 to 10 percent grade is usually considered steep. A rise of 3 to 7 percent is moderately hilly. A gentle rise is about 1 or 2 percent.

The steepest railroad track is around 3 percent, and roads that follow them are likely to be flat. Keep in mind that the road may climb or fall as it wanders away from the tracks. Or the train may go through a tunnel while the road goes up and over the top.

For some additional perspective, staircases are usually about 72 percent or between 30 and 35 degrees. At 77 percent or 40 degrees, hikers use both hands and feet to climb a hill. Wait a minute, that can't be right! I'm sure that nasty hill I rode the other day was at least as steep as a staircase!

Tunnels and Bridges

Tunnels can add an element of excitement to your tour; sometimes, too much excitement. Tunnels tend to be narrow and dark, and long ones can be dangerous to a bicyclist. We have traveled through some short tunnels in areas of little traffic and had no trouble. However, some tunnels are closed to cyclists.

Cyclists are forbidden to ride through the very long tunnel at Zion National Park in Utah. We hitched a ride on a passing pick-up truck. The rangers will also carry you through for a fee. In the U.S., there are enough people who drive trucks that it is not difficult to hitch a ride with someone. Another approach is to stop a passing car and ask for an "escort." Ask them to drive slowly behind you through the tunnel. If you have never done anything like this, it may seem bizarre, and it may seem bizarre to the person you stop. But take my word for it, someone will help you out. Humans have a worse reputation than they deserve.

Some tunnels that are closed to bicycles may have an alternate route around the tunnel. It is possible that you may have to come up with your own alternate plan.

The same caveat applies to bridges. In my home city of Philadelphia, bikes can ride the pedestrian walkway over the Ben

Franklin Bridge between Philadelphia and New Jersey, but they are forbidden on the Delaware Memorial Bridge.

If you see a tunnel or bridge on your route, try to find out about it ahead of time. You can contact local bike clubs, the department of transportation or the office of tourism. If you can't find information ahead of time, either plan another route or charge on ahead hoping for the best, but prepared to make a detour.

Paved and Unpaved Roads

I recommend eliminating any unpaved roads if you are planning your first tour.

Frequently, the unpaved roads look so inviting. On unpaved roads, there is less traffic — with good reason. They can seem so adventurous and scenic, and this is frequently the case. However, paved roads are a safer bet when you are unfamiliar with the area. It is much harder to estimate how far you can travel in a day on unpaved roads because they vary so much from one to another. The weather will also influence touring distance on unpaved roads much more than on paved roads.

I ride a road bike and have finally learned to be very cautious about unpaved roads. In Utah, we started off on a great, steep,

We read about the difficult conditions for bicycling in Iceland. Here the road crosses a shallow river.

hard-packed dirt road that went up between two passes. Zion National Park commanded the vista behind us. It was fabulous. And then the rain started. The mud was so thick and the clearance between my frame and the tire was so small that I couldn't ride the bike. I couldn't even push it for more than 10 yards before having to scrape mud out. Needless to say, this slowed us down quite a bit.

If you have a mountain bike or hybrid, these roads may be just what you are looking for. However, until you have some touring experience, it is best to have a paved alternate route chosen ahead of time. Also, be conservative in your planned daily mileage. The road may be more difficult than you anticipated and you may travel slower than you expected, if only to get off the bike and give your jangled bones a rest every half hour.

Other Features of the Terrain

From Death Valley to the Great Barrier Reef, people have a tendency to use descriptive names. There are many good guesses you can make from looking at the map. Summit Road is probably at the top of the hill, as is Ridge Ave. You will probably have to climb when you leave Pleasant Valley.

Water flows to the lowest possible point, taking the path of least resistance. That means that when you are approaching a body of water, there is a good chance you will be going downhill. A path that closely follows a river or creek is probably fairly flat. That doesn't mean it won't have a slight grade, however. Downhill and downstream are usually the same direction and you should expect at least a gradual incline over a long distance if you are going upriver. Of course, as soon as a path turns away from the water, expect a climb.

Don't expect roads that follow the coastline to be flat. One of Michael's first bike tours was along the Maine coast. His family always spent their summers at the New Jersey shore, which is as flat as a tabletop. He assumed that Maine's coastal roads would be the same as New Jersey's and was sorely mistaken. Or should I say he was sore and mistaken? New Jersey's coast is marsh and beaches. The Maine coast is lined with cliffs that charge up and down with great frequency. He planned long routes because he thought it would be an easy ride. Instead, he ended up pushing himself and his companion to the edge of their abilities (and sensibilities) in order to get back to the airport in time for their flight.

The lesson about checking the topography was not the only one he learned, however. In retrospect, he realized that he and his friend would have had a better time if they had called the airline, swallowed the rescheduling fee, and taken a flight the next day. They also could have waited in a town for a bus, or even called a cab. There is no point in making yourself miserable. Be flexible. If one plan isn't working out, make another one. The idea is to have fun.

Local Bike Routes and Bike Clubs

Look for bike paths when visiting cities. City streets can be unpleasant especially if you are unfamiliar with them. Most designated bike routes try to avoid the worst traffic and take cyclists through parks and other peaceful settings.

Contact a local bike club to find out about preferred routes. You can find bike clubs through the Yellow Pages or the Internet. There are many bicycle club Web pages. You can contact them via E-mail or the Internet to request information. Include in your query where you are going, listing specific places where you think you may have difficulty and ask for suggestions. I am a member of the Bicycling Club of Philadelphia. We get quite a few requests for information on biking in our area from tourists planning a visit. People love to give advice. It is fun for everyone involved and provides some very useful information.

Topographic Maps

To find out as much as you can about the hills on your proposed tour you will need to use a topographic map or "topo." I strongly recommend them unless you are very confident in your knowledge of the terrain.

Topographic maps show the contour of the land by using lines representing an incremental change in elevation. They are easy to use but it takes a little time to decipher the grade. A simple rule of thumb is that the more contour lines a road crosses, the steeper the hill. Look at the numbers shown on every few lines to determine if the hill goes up or down in your direction. Check the legend to see how much elevation each line represents. This varies a great deal between different topos. Crossing even one line may mean a nasty hill if the contour lines are every 1,000 feet. Maps suitable for cycling should have contour lines at least every 200 or 300 feet (about 70 to 100 meters).

Usually, mileage is not marked and you will need to measure that yourself. Don't forget to add a bit to the total in very hilly areas to account for rise and fall.

Large-Scale Maps

If you cannot get topos, at least try to get a large-scale map. Some, but not all road maps tell you the scale. Look for the scale of miles. Somewhere near it, usually right above it, you will find a number that says "1 : some big number." This is the scale the map is drawn to. Typical roads maps are drawn to a scale of 1 : 1,000,000 to 1 : 3,000,000. This means that a centimeter is equal to about 10 kilometers and an inch is equal to about 15 miles, for 1 : 1,000,000. A centimeter is equal to about 30 km and an inch is equal to about 45 miles at 1 : 3,000,000.

Most topo maps are drawn to a large enough scale to provide excellent detail even on very twisty roads. For touring, try to get maps with a scale of 1 : 100,000 to 1 : 500,000. Maps with a scale larger than 1 : 100,000 will be too big and cumbersome for most cyclotourists. Scales smaller than 1 : 500,000 do not show enough detail. On a map with a scale of 1 : 100,000, an inch equals about 1.5 miles and a centimeter is about 1 km. For a scale of 1 : 500,000, an inch is 7.5 miles and a centimeter is about 5 km.

Software

There are several mapping computer programs. They vary in cost and quality. Generally those that are easier to use are less powerful and flexible. The ones that can do the most tricks tend to be more complicated and take longer to learn. My favorite is DeLorme's Topo USA. I have also used Microsoft's Streets which is very easy to learn but limited in its capabilities. For example, there is no topography and it is hard or impossible to modify routes. Topo USA shows a topographic profile, allows you to modify routes and transfer your chosen route directly into a cue sheet. However, it is cumbersome and takes time to learn. Topo!, another program, seems to be similar to Topo USA but I am not familiar with it.

Modifying Someone Else's Route

Pre-fab routes are great starting points for designing your own tour but don't limit yourself to the provided route. It is easy to change them to suit your own needs by using the methods described in this book. Use the routes suggested as starting points. Then detour to cover places you want to go or to avoid places that don't interest you. And you don't have to ride the same number of miles or days as the book's route.

You Still Need a Good Map!

Whether you use the prescribed route exactly as suggested or adapt it to your own desires, you should always carry a detailed, up-to-date map. The instructions almost never include other roads in the area and there is little or no information about towns and cities off the route. This information is important, however. You may need facilities that are within easy reach but are not listed. Also, everyone gets lost at least once. With a map, you can get yourself right back on the route with only a minor delay. Without one, you might be a block away and you would never know.

I have cycled into an area that looked great on the map but found it to be dangerous, closed for construction or unpleasant in some other way. With a map in my hand, I can easily plot a detour.

Photocopying Maps

Most maps do not photocopy well. The details are frequently lost. This is especially true of topographic maps. This makes photocopies unreliable for planning a trip. I could not find accurate, detailed maps of Cuba until I found a ten-year-old atlas in a library. Since I could not take it with me, I had no choice but to use a photocopy. I had enough information that we knew approximately what to expect, but my mileage estimates were almost all incorrect by about ten percent. I also needed to gather information from less accurate, but more recent, road maps.

However, once you have decided on your route, a photocopy can be an asset on the tour. You can mark the photocopy, outlining the route, highlighting sites, and making notes, without marring your original. If you will only be using a part of a large map, you can photocopy one section. Then you will have a single 8 ½ x 11 inch piece of paper instead of a bulky map to place in your map holder. This is especially helpful if you are using a map from a book. It isn't easy to squish a book into one of those little plastic holders!

Always bring the original map with you. You can keep it inside your pack, where it is less likely to be damaged by exposure to the elements, but you will probably want it for reference. Making a couple of copies will safeguard against losing or damaging the first photocopy.

Closing Notes

1. It is better to plan a distance that is too short than one that is too long. You can always continue pedaling and travel farther. Or you can stop early and find some mischief to get into for the rest of the day. Some days you will have less flexibility than others. When you have several choices, write them in your notes. These days will be your buffer if the situation is different than you expected.

2. The most important lesson to learn from this chapter is this: Don't become so committed to a route that you won't consider alternatives if you find the situation is less than ideal. The flexible traveler is a happy traveler.

Don't expect roads that follow coastlines to be flat.

5.

Teaching by Example

Pat's Tour of the Northern California Coast

IN this chapter, I will show you step by step how I planned the route for a tour of the northern California coast that Michael and I took recently. I will not go into detail about each turn we made, or give precise directions and distances. I am not giving you a tour route you can take yourself, although you can do that if you want. You will need to read about the area, get a couple of maps, and adapt my trip to your tastes. What I want to show you is an example of the process we have discussed in the preceding chapters. Starting after I picked out my destination, I will take you through my selection of books, maps, and roads and give you the reasons for my final route and itinerary.

Then I will compare that to the one we actually took. I will discuss the reasons we changed our route and the options we considered.

We decided to fly to San Francisco and head north in a circle route. We looked through a brochure from a company that organizes group cycling tours and made some notes. The tour through the Napa Valley, wine country, sounded good, as did a trip along the coast. The coastal route boasted wonderful giant redwood trees and dramatic coastline. Although Michael visited San Francisco when he was a teenager, I had never been there and I was looking forward to spending a couple of days seeing the city.

Timing

We had three weeks altogether and figured we would spend about fourteen days cycling. This would give us two full days for travel and packing and unpacking our bikes and gear. We would have a couple of days in San Francisco and a couple more "floaters" during the tour to give us some flexibility. Our estimated daily distance was 50 miles. Fifty miles a day for two weeks gave us a total of about 700 miles. A quick look at a road map showed that the city of Eureka is about 350 miles north of San Francisco. That became my initial turn-around point.

I went to the bookstore and looked for books on cycling in the area. I found *Bicycling the Pacific Coast* by Tom Kirkendall and Vicky Spring. Almost immediately, the authors talked about the strong prevailing northerly winds, so I decided to go inland when we biked north from San Francisco. This would put wine country first on our itinerary. We could continue north and at some point in the redwood forests we would turn around and go south along the coast, enjoying the tail wind.

Are There Roads in the Area That Are Suitable for Cycling?

As I scanned the map, I noticed that there are very few inland alternatives to Highway 101 north of the Napa Valley to the redwoods. I needed to find out if this stretch of highway is acceptable for cycling.

Bicycling the Pacific Coast includes the section of Highway 101 from the redwood forests to Eureka, so I was reassured. I found out through Caltrans, the department of transportation in California, that bicycles are allowed on Highway 101 where there was no alternate through road.

Gathering Information

I needed more information about the area to fill in the details so I started collecting books and maps. In addition to *Bicycling the Pacific Coast*, I bought *Hidden San Francisco and Northern California* by Ray Riegert, *Northern California Coast Best Places* by Matthew R. Poole, and *Lonely Planet's City Guide to San Francisco* by Tony Wheeler. I borrowed *Fodor's Campground Directory for Northern California* from a friend and photocopied the relevant pages. The DeLorme series of *Atlases and Gazetteers* is an excellent source of topographic maps for the United

States and I bought the Northern California edition. Adventure Cycling prints detailed annotated maps of many cross-country routes in the U.S. The routes are broken up into small sections and you can buy a map for each section. They have a route from Vancouver to San Diego and I bought a map for the section between Crescent City, north of Eureka, and San Francisco. I also had a department of tourism road map of California. The total cost for this library of information was $84.

Was all of this necessary? No. Only a detailed map of the area is essential. If I wanted to carry only one book, it would be the Atlas and Gazetteer. With this I could navigate the route and at least make a prediction about the facilities available in towns based on the amount of

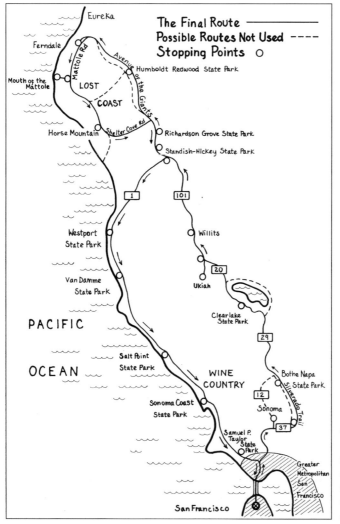

Fig. 5.1.
This is my final planned route. I included a couple of alternatives as well.

development shown on the map. However, I am not willing to leave everything up to chance. I wanted to have at least a few listings of available camping and lodging.

On this particular trip, the most helpful books were the campground directory and the guide to San Francisco. I could have gotten along without the *Hidden* and the *Best Places* books.

As I read, I learned about an area called "The Lost Coast." This region is west of Humboldt Redwood State Park and south of Eureka. The terrain is too rough for a highway and is largely undeveloped. It sounded intriguing. Most of the area we would cover is popular with motorists and cyclists and it would be nice to get off the beaten track for a bit.

At this point, I had a rough plan: San Francisco to the Napa Valley to Humboldt Redwoods State Park to Eureka to the Lost Coast to the "found" coast to San Francisco. I reserved our flights and began to make up our itinerary. Figure 5-1 shows our final plan. You can refer to it as you read.

Our Planned Itinerary

Day 1: Wednesday August 27

Fly from Philadelphia to San Francisco. We were scheduled to arrive in San Francisco around noon. This would give us time to put our bikes and gear together and then spend the evening around town.

Day 2: Thursday, August 28

Through San Francisco on Adventure Cycling's route. Use city map to navigate to Highway 37 to Highway 121 to Sonoma. 53 miles.

I planned to begin cycling the following day. Our destination was easy to decide. Traveling north out of San Francisco on inland roads, the first town with overnight lodging is Sonoma, 53 miles from San Francisco. That should be a comfortable cycling distance, and since it was in wine country, it was on our list of places to go.

We would travel through the San Francisco suburbs for about half that distance. The map from Adventure Cycling would lead us most of the way and it looked as if we would be able to navigate from there out to the highway that leads to Sonoma by using a detailed city map.

Bicycling in a city that is unfamiliar is time-consuming and requires patience. Keeping this in mind, we would start off early. I also made reservations at a hotel in Sonoma before we left home. This allowed us to arrive after dark if necessary and we would not worry about finding a place to stay or putting up the tent in the dark.

Day 3: Friday, August 29

Sonoma to Napa on route 121 and north on the Silverado Trail to Bothe-Napa State Park. 43 miles. Figure 5.2.

I saw two options for going through wine country. We could backtrack a few miles and then ride east to Napa and north through the Napa Valley. The Silverado Trail runs parallel to Highway 29 through the Napa Valley. I learned that this is road was very good for cycling and it is listed as a scenic route.

On the other hand, route 12 goes north from Sonoma. The road is hillier and we would need to bike up and over the ridge that separated the Sonoma and Napa Valleys. However, it is shorter and most advice says that it is more scenic.

My final decision was made based on the location of Bothe-Napa State Park on the northern end of the Silverado Trail. The campground directory gave it an excellent rating and it has a swimming pool. It is located 43 miles from Sonoma. The Silverado Trail and Napa Valley won.

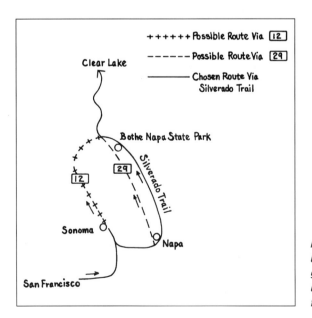

Fig. 5.2.
We had two options to get from Sonoma to Clear Lake. We chose the Silverado Trail.

Day 4: Saturday, August 30

North on Route 29 from Bothe-Napa State Park to Clear Lake State Park. 55 miles. Figure 5.3.

    Staying inland and staying off Highway 101 for as long as possible meant riding north on route 29 to Clear Lake. Luckily, this is a scenic route that has little traffic. My topographic map told me that we would be climbing a long steep hill less than an hour out of Both-Napa State Park. That is OK, we would be fresh and rested. After a short down hill, the road is flat to Clear Lake.

    At that point, I needed to decide whether to go around the lake on the north or the south road. Both are marked as scenic routes. The north route looked fairly flat according to the topo. My campground directory indicated commercial campgrounds at the northwest end of the lake. The biggest disadvantage to the north route is a nine-mile stretch of divided highway that we needed to traverse. It also looks like more traffic funnels into the north road.

    By contrast, the southerly route is hilly. The advantages are less traffic and a state park with an excellent rating 55 miles from Bothe-Napa. The location of the park and the divided highway lead me to choose the southerly route.

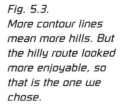

Fig. 5.3.
More contour lines mean more hills. But the hilly route looked more enjoyable, so that is the one we chose.

Day 5: Sunday, August 31

West on 29 from Clear Lake State Park to route 20. West on 20 to 101. North on 101 to Willits. 55 miles.

The scenic route continues around the lake and then heads west, ending where route 29 meets route 20. As much as I wanted to avoid riding on highway 101, it looked like it was necessary if I wanted to reach the redwood forests. There are roads that head into the national forests but they were unpaved after a few miles. Plus the routes they take are very hilly and circuitous. It is much longer and our pace would be slower than on 101. I was resigned to head west on route 20 and to join 101 and go north.

Willits is a medium size town 55 miles away from Clear Lake State Park According to my guidebooks, we should be able to find lodging, restaurants and grocery stores.

Day 6: Monday, September 1

North on 101 from Willits to Standish-Hickey Recreation Area. 45 miles.

Forty-five miles from Willits, we would arrive at Standish- Hickey, the first state recreation area in the redwoods. There is a campground there., making it my choice of destination for the day.

Day 7: Tuesday, September 2

Highway 101 to "The Avenue of the Giants" and on to Humboldt Redwoods State Park. 50 miles.

It is fifty miles to Humboldt Redwoods State Park. About halfway, we could leave Highway 101 and ride on a parallel secondary road called "The Avenue of the Giants." This road might have some tourist traffic, but all of the through traffic, including commercial trucking would stay on 101.

Day 8: Wednesday, September 3

Stay in Humboldt State Park. 0 miles.

I expected this state park to be very nice. It is highly recommended by my camping guide and the Kirkendall book. I wanted to plan at least two days along the way when we would not be biking. This seemed like a good place for day hiking and loafing.

Day 9: Thursday, September 4

Humboldt Redwood State Park to Fortuna along The Avenue of the Giants and Highway 101. Then the Mattole Road into Ferndale. 35 miles. Figure 5.4.

At that point, we would leave the state parks and recreation areas. We would be able to stay on The Avenue of the Giants for about ten miles and then rejoin highway 101.

Friday was the start of Labor Day weekend and it would be difficult to assure a place to stay either in campgrounds or hotels. I thought that the Lost Coast would have much less tourist traffic than the surrounding areas, so I wanted to spend the coming weekend there. That meant that I should be at one of the three access roads by Thursday night. Ferndale is only about 35 miles from Humboldt Redwoods State Park and is located at the north access road. It looked like it would be a good idea to stop heading north in Fortuna and turn west on the Mattole Road into Ferndale instead of going all the way up to Eureka. My guidebooks indicated that there were a few hotels in Ferndale, but no campground. A hotel would be a nice change of pace.

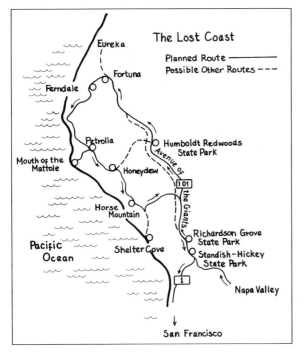

Fig. 5.4.
We planned to turn west in Fortuna to tour through the Lost Coast.

Day 10: Friday, September 5

Mattole Road from Ferndale to Petrolia. Mouth of the Mattole Road to beach campground. 55 miles.

We would leave Ferndale on the Mattole Road riding up into the Lost Coast. About fifty miles from Ferndale is the tiny town of Petrolia. My books said there is a small store. Even if the store was closed, there is a guest house as well where we should be able to get water at least. At Petrolia we could turn west and go down the Mouth of the Mattole Road to the coast where there is a primitive state campground. We would need to have food and water to get us through the day and the night. The campground is right on the beach and was usually deserted. Sounded lovely.

Day 11: Saturday, September 6

Mouth of the Mattole Campground. 0 miles.

In fact, it sounded so nice that I thought we would stay an extra day. If all went well, we could spend a day listening to the waves crash. We would need to be sure to carry enough food and water from Ferndale for two days.

The Lost Coast is very rugged and hilly. It was possible that we would cover fewer miles than usual. Having planned an extra day at the campsite gave us time to stretch out this section into more days with fewer miles per day. In addition to the store in Petrolia, there is a store in Honeydew, less than ten miles away. I thought this was enough assurance that we would be able to find food and water. There were a few scattered homesteads along the way as well where we should be able to get water. I was a little concerned about the remoteness of the area and needed to get more information about the availability of food and water when we arrived in California. There was always the possibility of going only as far as Petrolia and then going back to Ferndale if we find we cannot get everything we needed for the extra day.

Day 12: Sunday, September 7

Mouth of the Mattole campground to Petrolia on the Mouth of the Mattole Road. Petrolia to Honeydew on the Mattole Road. Honeydew to Horse Mountain on the Horse Mountain Road. 25 miles.

It is only about 55 miles from the Mouth of the Mattole Campground back to highway 101 in the middle of the redwood forests.

However, it would be a tough 55 miles beginning with the climb up from the beach. There is another primitive state campground on Horse Mountain, about 25 miles from Mouth of the Mattole. We would pass Honeydew, with a store, along the way.

It was also still Labor Day weekend. Splitting the return leg into two days would bring us out onto the main highway on Monday, after the weekend campers left.

Day 13: Monday, September 8

Horse Mountain campground to the Sheltercove Road. Then to highway 101 on the Sheltercove Road. Highway 101 to Richardson Grove State Park. 50 miles.

Highway 101 is about thirty miles away. The trip from Horse Mountain campground would be mostly down hill. It is another fairly flat twenty miles south on highway 101 to Richardson Grove State Park. We would backtrack for part of highway 101. However, I did not see another alternative because there were so few roads in the area.

Shade from the Giant Redwoods helped, but it was still too hot for me in northern California.

Day 14: Tuesday, September 9

Highway 101 from Richardson Grove State Park to highway 1. Then take highway 1 west to the coast. Continue south to Westport State Park. 54 miles.

We would continue to backtrack along Highway 101 until we reached Highway 1 where we would jut out to the west and travel south along the coast. We could follow Highway 1 most of the way to San Francisco. For the next few days, I would not have to figure out which road to use, just how many miles to go. After Richardson Grove, the next state park was Westport, about 54 miles away. Just right.

Day 15: Wednesday, September 10

Highway 1 from Westport to Van Damme State Park. 27 miles.

Westport is less than two hundred miles from San Francisco. I wanted to arrive in San Francisco on Sunday, in five days. I could either shorten my days a bit or spend an extra day on the coast. Or I could arrive in San Francisco early. After looking at the campgrounds that would be available along the coast, I decided to shorten two days. We would bike 27 miles to Van Damme State Park.

Day 16: Thursday, September 11

Highway 1 from Van Damme to Salt Point State Park. 54 miles.

A friend of mine stayed in Salt Point State Park and loved it. It is remote and beautiful and 54 miles from Van Damme.

Day 17: Friday, September 12

Highway 1 from Salt Point to Sonoma Coast State Park. 27 miles.

We could spend extra time in Salt Point if we planned a shorter biking day. Sonoma Coast State Park is 27 miles from Salt Point.

Day 18: Saturday, September 13

Highway 1 from Sonoma Coast to Samuel P. Taylor State Park. 40 miles.

San Francisco is now about 80 miles away and, as luck would have it, Samuel P. Taylor State Park is about half way.

Day 19: Sunday, September 14

Adventure Cycling route to San Francisco. 40 miles.

We would ride along the route described in Adventure Cycling's map. This would take us across the Golden Gate Bridge. We had the Lonely Planet Guide to San Francisco to take us to our hotel.

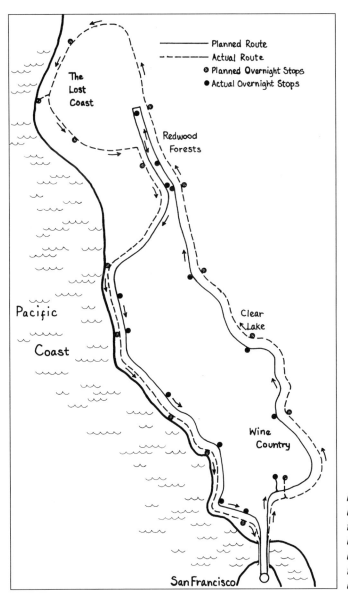

Fig. 5.5.
We never did go to the Lost Coast because of the heat and the uncertainty of finding water.

Days 20, 21: September 15 and 16

In San Francisco. 0 miles.

We would spend the next two days in San Francisco before returning to Philadelphia on Tuesday, September 17.

The Best Laid Plans of Mice and Men...: What Really Happened

Now let's look at the actual route we took. (Figure 5.5)

What you will notice when you compare the two routes is that we never got to the Lost Coast. The problem was the weather. We encountered record high temperatures, over 100 degrees Fahrenheit, for a week from Bothe-Napa State Park on. We wanted to head to the coast sooner than planned to escape the heat. I was also concerned because the Lost Coast is so remote. We were each drinking between one and two gallons of fluids each day in the heat and there was no way we could carry that much liquid with us. In addition to the two small towns of Petrolia and Honeydew, there were a couple of campgrounds in the state forest that was part of the Lost Coast. If I had not felt so much like a fried egg, I would have been willing to try. But we felt it would be uncomfortable at best and a health risk at worst. So we pointed our bikes south and headed into the cool fog of the coast. That threw off our planned itinerary down the coast, but we knew which road to take, we had a campground directory and we had plenty of time to get to San Francisco. We decided how far we would travel each morning when we started out.

When we decided to change the route, we had to come up with an alternative plan. We had several options: We could add a loop of cycling north of San Francisco We could continue south of San Francisco for a while. We could spend more days in San Francisco. We could stop at some of the coastal towns and spend a day or two on the beach. Or we could rent a car when we got back to San Francisco and drive out to Yosemite National Park for a couple of days, which is what we did. Sometimes a change of plans leads to an unexpected pleasure. Yosemite was beautiful and I am very glad we were able to see it.

Part II.

Packing Your Bike

6.

Your Touring Bike

WHICH bicycle is best? In most cases, the best bike to take on your first tour is the one you already own. Do not run out and buy a bike that is specifically designed for touring until you have tried it a few times. Your opinions may change as you get more experience. You may find that you prefer road touring to off-road. Or you may decide to do lots of rugged mountain biking. There is even the tiniest teeniest possibility that you do not want to tour at all. Before you toss down large sums of money, try taking a trip or two on your current bicycle.

In the meantime, you should familiarize yourself with bikes in general and your bike in specific. This chapter is an introduction to the basic anatomy and physiology of bicycles. We will also go over some of the features that are an asset in a touring bike. You can adapt your bike to some of these and they are also options to look for if you decide to buy a touring bike.

Almost all of what I know about bicycle mechanics I learned by disassembling my own bike, packing it up, and reassembling it for tours. When Michael and I began using boxes, I knew very little. By observing at first, then assisting, and finally doing it myself, I have vastly improved my understanding of bicycles. Disassembling and assembling the bike also allows me to give the bike a thorough check-up before the tour to be sure that it is in good working order.

Just as importantly, if you take your bike apart before you tour, you will know absolutely that you have all of the tools that you will need to service it on the road.

Figure 6.1 shows some of the basic parts of a typical bike. Other figures will show details when I think they will be helpful.

Is Your Bike Adequate?

To take your first tour, any general purpose road, mountain bike (all terrain or mountain) or hybrid bike that is in good working order is adequate. The exceptions are bicycles that are highly specialized for uses other than touring. For example, BMX, track, and triathlon bikes are poor choices. However, if you own one of these bikes, chances are that you know enough about biking to make a good choice. You probably do not want to head off across the country on a unicycle or a bike with a banana seat and high-rise handle bars either.

Try your bike out on a few overnight trips, carrying packs. Travel the same distances that you expect to cover on your tour and bike on roads that have about the same kinds of hills. If you are comfortable on these trips, you will be fine on your tour. Even a three- or five-speed bike is OK as long as you travel short distances (20–25 miles a day) and stay on fairly flat roads.

① Saddle
② Rear Rack
③ Rear Wheel
④ Rear Rim
⑤ Rear Derailleur
⑥ Chain
⑦ Chain Stay
⑧ Chain Rings
⑨ Crank Arm
⑩ Pedal
⑪ Toe Clip
⑫ Front Derailleur
⑬ Seat Stay
⑭ Rear Brakes
⑮ Seat Post
⑯ Seat Tube
⑰ Frame Pump
⑱ Front Drop Out
⑲ Front Hub
⑳ Front Rack
㉑ Shifters
㉒ Brake Lever
㉓ Brake Cables
㉔ Handlebars
㉕ Stem
㉖ Head Set
㉗ Top Tube
㉘ Water Bottle Cages
㉙ Front Tube
㉚ Front Brake
㉛ Fork
㉜ Gears
㉝ Spokes
㉞ Nipples

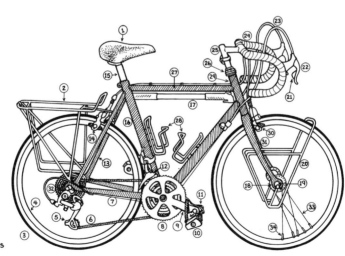

Fig. 6.1 The touring bike, with the individual parts identified.

Bike Fit

Make sure your bike is the right size. When you stand straddling a road or hybrid bike, your crotch should clear the top tube by at least an inch. Mountain bikes should give you at least two inches of clearance.

The Saddle

Having the right saddle, properly adjusted for you, is probably the most important factor in making your bike comfortable. Sitting on the saddle, push one pedal down until it is at the lowest possible point. Put your heel on the pedal. Your leg should be fully extended without straining to reach the pedal. If you cannot touch the pedal with your heel, your saddle is too high. If your leg is not fully extended, your saddle is too low. It is estimated that most recreational cyclists have positioned their saddles too low. This is one of the most common causes of knee pain among bikers.

The saddle can also be adjusted in two other ways. You can move it closer or further away from the handlebars and adjust the angle of the horn up or down relative to the seat. You can move the saddle forward if feel like you are reaching too far for the handlebars or back further if you feel like you are too close.

If your saddle is angled with the front too high, it will be very uncomfortable. This is very irritating for anyone and is a major cause of penile numbness among men. If it is angled with the front too low, you will feel like you are sliding off toward the front. Since these adjustments are easy to correct, you can feel free to try several different positions until you find one that is just right.

Handlebars

The handlebars can also be adjusted easily. In addition to adjusting the height, you can also turn the handlebars upward or downward to increase your comfort. As with the saddle, try different positions until you decide on the most comfortable one.

You should not be able to move the handlebars or the saddle by hand without a lot of effort.

What to Look for Before Your Trip

Once you have adjusted the bike to fit you comfortably, you should make sure it is in good working order. Check the nuts, bolts, and screws, and make sure everything is tightened. Your bike shouldn't make any noise when you ride. If it rattles, scrapes, grinds, squeaks or goes bump in the night, try to find out where the noise is coming from and get it fixed.

Chain

The chain needs to be oiled often. Any lubricant will do from sewing machine oil to spray lubricants and so-called dry lubricants. Some will last longer than others and there are many bikers who will wax poetic about waxing your chain if you have the interest in listening to them. Do what you think is best, but be sure you put something on the chain frequently to keep it moving smoothly and to prevent rust.

Cleaning the Bike

Rust and road crud are unwelcome on your bike. Of course, the bike is going to get dirty. But you want to try to keep greasy chunks from clogging things up. Occasional attention to the derailleurs and brakes will help even if you only knock off the big stuff.

Rust can form on the brake and derailleur cables causing them to stick. If your cables seem to be moving easily, no problem. If they are not, try squirting some oil down the cable housing and moving the cable back and forth to loosen it. If that does not work, you may need to take it in to the shop for some expert help.

Wheels

Check the wheel bearings by trying to wiggle the wheels from side to side. There should be no play. If there is, take it to a bike shop.

Your wheels should be "true," that is, they should turn in a smooth circle without wobbling or rubbing on the frame or the brakes. There should be no missing, bent, broken or rusted spokes. If the wheel is out of true or there are spokes that need to be replaced, fix it before your tour. It is easy to true a wheel and it takes only a little practice to replace spokes on the front wheel or on the side of the rear wheel that is opposite the gears.

Broken Spokes

If you break a spoke on the road and either do not have a replacement or need to keeping traveling, you can true the wheel and replace the spoke later. Remove the broken spoke first. If you leave it on, it can get stuck in the wheel, the derailleur or the packs. You can ride like this for the rest of the day if your other spokes are in good condition. The one time I broke a spoke on a tour, I finished the trip and replaced it when I returned home. However, the sooner you replace the broken spoke, the better. Eventually, the stress on the remaining spokes will cause another one to break.

The increased weight of touring packs makes the rear wheel more vulnerable to broken spokes. In all bikes, spokes fatigue with use and age. Frequently, the whole wheel experiences stress at the same time, which means you could pop more than one on a trip. If this happens, take the wheel to a bike shop as soon as you can. It may be possible to rebuild the wheel or you may need to buy a new one.

On our tour of California, Michael broke a total of four spokes. All of these were on the rear wheel. We replaced the first but then we had no more spares. A few days later he popped another one. It is not good to have broken spokes on the rear wheel with the weight of the packs, so he took one from the front. And then he lost one more. And then the fourth. He finished the last three days of our trip with one spoke missing in the back and two missing in the front.

Why did this happen? Partly because it was a lousy wheel to start with, partly because of the weight and partly because the wheel had seen a lot of heavy use in its life. You are much less likely to have problems with your spokes if you begin with a true wheel in good condition. Other than this one anomaly, we have collectively broken only one spoke in thousands of touring miles, so don't think you can use this story as an excuse for staying home! By the way, we now carry three spare spokes.

Tires

Check your tires before you begin your tour. They should have no slashes, worn spots or dry rot. The tread should be in good condition. Replace them if necessary.

I hope it is obvious that you should keep your tires inflated to the proper pressure. Over-inflated tires are more likely to blow out, give a hard ride and make steering over-responsive or skittish. Under-inflated tires will slow you down, are more likely to develop pinch flats and make the bike less responsive. Riding on seriously low tires can damage the wheel rim. In any case, the tires will wear out faster.

Inner Tubes

You should always carry a new spare inner tube or two. Check the size of your tire and be sure the spare tube fits. You must have the right wheel size, that is, 26-inch, 27-inch, 650 C or 700 C. These are measurements of the approximate diameter of the wheel. However, you can use a slightly fatter tube than your tire so you can use a tire size 34 C tube in a 32 C tire.

Also be sure you are getting the right valve. There are two types: Presta and Schrader. Metric wheels tend to have Presta valves. Wheels measured in inches tend to use Schraders. You can use a Presta in a wheel that was built for a Schrader because the Presta valve is smaller, however, a Schrader valve will not fit on a wheel meant for Prestas. Most bike pumps will adapt to either Presta or Schrader. When you buy the pump, ask the salesperson to show you how to convert from one to the other.

Flat tires are a way of life for bicyclists. Everyone who rides should know how to fix a flat whether you are biking five or a hundred miles. You can decrease your flat tire episodes with thin plastic liners inserted between the inner tube and the wheel rim. These are available in many sizes. There are also tires that have some kind of reinforcing built into the tire wall. One of the best materials for this is Kevlar.

Gears

Check the gear cables to make sure they are not frayed or cracked. The housing should not have kinks or breaks. If the cables feel sticky, a couple of drops of oil squirted down the housing may be all that is needed to loosen them.

You should be able to use all of your rear cogs and all of your front chainrings. You should be able to shift smoothly. If you have indexed shifting, you should be able to push a button or turn a lever or knob and the bike should shift without fussing. Your gears should not make any noise once you have shifted.

Your chain should not slip off the cogs and chainrings either to the inside or the outside. This does happen once in a while, especially when you are riding hard or shifting quickly through several gears. (You can put the chain back on by shifting to the previous gear.) However, if your bike does this frequently, you need to adjust the derailleur limits. I will not discuss this in the next chapter since it does not need to be done regularly. If you have this problem, take the bike to a shop and they can adjust it for you for a small fee.

Theoretically, you should be able to use all of the gear combinations without the chain and derailleur rubbing. In practice, however, this may not be the case. The rings and cogs are layered. The easiest gears are closest to the bike frame. The hardest gears are the farthest away. So when you are in your easiest rear cog and your easiest

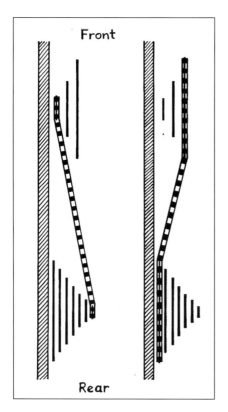

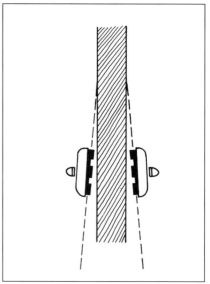

Left: Fig. 6.2. This is an example of extreme gearing: using the easiest chainring with the hardest rear cog or vice versa. This twists the chain, so you should avoid it.

Below: Fig. 6.3. Brake pads should be "toed-in"— the front of the pad should contact the rim of the wheel slightly before the rear.

front chainring, the chain is close to the bike. In the hardest cog and hardest chainring, the chain is farther away. If you use the easiest chainring with the hardest rear cog, the chain is close to the frame in the front and far away from the frame in the back. Some bikes are able to handle this, but none of them really like it. The chain is twisted and trying to roll on an angle (Figure 6.2) This will cause many chains and derailleurs to rub against each other. Try to avoid this. Shift to a harder chainring before you are in the hardest rear gear and to an easier chainring before you are in the easiest rear gear.

This means that you really do not have a full 27 gears on a bike with three chainrings and nine rear gears. However, it is still better than the typical ten-speed, because the range from your easiest gear to your hardest gear is much wider. Those gears that you will not use are in the middle of the two extremes and are easily substituted by a different combination of gears.

Brakes

Check the brakes. As with gear cables, your brake cables should be in good condition and should move freely. You brakes should not feel sticky.

Do the levers move easily? Squeeze them hard. The brakes should be fully engaged before you have squeezed the levers all the way to the handlebars. In other words, there should still be room to pull the levers further in, but you cannot because the brake pads are pushed as hard as possible against the rims of the wheels. At the same time, you should be able to squeeze the levers just a little bit without having the brake pads pushed fully against the rims.

The brake pads should not look worn. They should be flat and should have tread. The pads should be adjusted so that they press right in the middle of the rim. It is dangerous if your brake pads are off the rim either onto the tire or below the rim towards the spokes. Both sides of the brakes should apply pressure to the rim with the same force, at the same time.

The pads should be "toed in" slightly, meaning that they should engage toward the front of the pad first. Figure 6.3 shows how this looks. Squealing brakes are usually caused by improper alignment. Toeing them in a little will stop the noise. I hope everyone reading this does not need to be told that you should never lubricate your brake pads.

Cranks and Pedals

Your pedals should rotate smoothly and noiselessly. The pedals are attached to the crank arms which are attached to the bottom bracket. The bottom bracket is the axle for the pedals. This is where the power of your legs is transmitted to the bike. There should be no play in the pedals, crank arms or bottom bracket.

Toeclips and Cleats

I recommend using cleats (clipless pedals) or toeclips for touring. (Figure 6.4) You will have more power and use less energy which is always helpful going up hills. I use cleats all the time now. However, I toured for thousands of miles with toeclips. These are inexpensive and easy to put on most pedals. The metal or plastic clip screws onto the front of the pedal and the strap just attaches through slots on the side.

Headsets

The headset is what connects your steering components (the fork and handlebars) to the frame, so it is important that it is properly adjusted. If the handlebars are hard to turn or are sticky, the headset may be too tight, which could damage the bearings. If it is too loose, it is dangerous. To check if your headset is loose, straddle the bike. Hold onto the handlebars and press the front brakes to prevent the wheel from rolling.

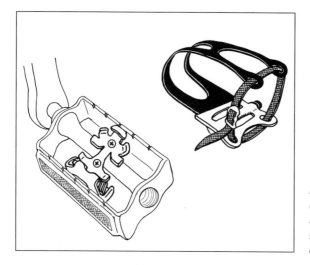

Fig. 6.4.
Using cleats, on the left, or toeclips makes your pedal strokes more efficient.

Then rapidly pull the handlebars back and forth (toward and away from you). If it is too loose, you will feel the tube inside moving around and it will definitely feel "wrong." If this is the case, you should tighten by hand the lower nut and then the upper nut. Then you should take the bike to a mechanic right away. This is a simple adjustment that will only take a moment but it needs to be done correctly. Adjusting the headset requires a "feel" that can be learned only by experience.

Racks

If you have a rack attached to the back of your bike, make sure it is in good condition. It should be bolted securely and should have no cracks, bends, rust or other evidence of damage. The rack should not move if you try to wiggle it. Most racks are capable of handling most touring loads, but make sure you are using a rack that is rated for the weights you are carrying, especially if you are carrying camping gear or other heavy loads.

If you do not have a rack, first make sure you can attach one. You will need eyelets or little holes on the frame near your rear hub. If you want to use front packs, you will need eyelets on the fork where the front wheel attaches. Braze-ons make it easier to attach your rack, but they are not necessary. These are factory installed screw holes in the frame. Braze-ons also allow you to attach water bottles and other accouterments.

Some racks are made specifically for road or mountain bikes, so make sure you purchase a rack that will work on your bike. Ask the salesperson about this when you buy it. The safest way is to bring your bike with you, but a knowledgeable salesperson should know what you need if you tell them the kind of bike you have.

Racks for Bikes with Suspension

Bicycles with suspension systems, or shock absorbers, usually need special racks that attach only to the seatpost or its equivalent. Shock absorbers on the wheels, both front and rear, allow the frame and wheels to move more independently, giving you a smoother ride. However, conventional racks are attached to both the wheel and the frame. Riding this way on a bike with a suspension system will cause the rack and anything on them to flex every time you hit a bump. The rack may negate the value of the shock absorbers or eventually, the rack may even break.

Ways to Improve Your Current Bike or to Consider for Your Next Bike

You and Your Saddle

Be sure your saddle fits your derriere. Until recently, most saddles were designed for men and comfort was last on the list of priorities. Long-distance cyclists look for a softer saddle and many women are more comfortable on a wider, shorter saddle. Now there are many choices available for both men and women. You will find styles that are better for different riding positions as well as several that are designed to minimize penile numbness. Some saddles have gel pads built in or you can buy a gel pad cover. When you are considering buying a new saddle, the shop should allow you to attach it to a bike in the store so your tush and the saddle can be properly introduced before the wedding.

Sometimes an uncomfortable saddle simply needs to be adjusted, so do not be shy about moving yours around a bit to see if that helps.

A good saddle is so important to your overall comfort while riding that it is always worth it to chuck the old one and buy a new one if it is not just right.

Tires

Do not bother to buy new tires for your first tour if your current ones are in good shape, but when you need to, you can get new ones easily and fairly inexpensively. Wider tires are better for touring bikes. Skinny, high-pressure tires are more prone to flats that wider, lower pressure tires. But you do not want the fat knobby ones on most mountain bikes. These just increase the road friction, slowing you down unnecessarily. They also emit an annoying buzz on the road. There is a new design developed for mountain bikes that works well for touring. It's called an inverted design. The middle of the tread is smooth, giving a nice ride on the road, but the edges of the tread are knobby. This way, if your tire sinks into dirt, gravel or mud, the knobby tread can grip better and give you the traction you need.

A good size for touring is about 1½ inches on 26-inch wheels and about 32 mm on 700 C wheels.

Wheels

Most wheels will handle more than one tire size. However, you may be limited. If you have very skinny wheels that will not take wide tires, you might want to consider different wheels at some point. Also, some wheels are stronger than others, some are made to carry heavy loads, and some are built for speed. For a touring bike, you should be more concerned about weight bearing capability. You can buy wheels that have more than the usual number of spokes (36 vs. 32). My road bike limits me to fairly skinny wheels and tires, and yours may too, so bring your bike with you and try the wheel and tire out before you buy it.

Gears

A nice wide range of gears, including some designed for hill climbing, will make your life much more pleasant. The big chainring is for fast, hard riding and the small one is for slow, easy riding and climbing hills. The opposite is true of the rear gears.

Mountain bikes usually have good hill climbing gears, but many road bikes and some hybrids do not. It is very difficult and sometimes impossible to convert a two-chainring bike to three chainrings. On the other hand, increasing the size of your rear gears is not as hard. You should have this done in a shop if you are not familiar with bike mechanics. You want to be sure your current derailleur can handle the new gears. If you have to get a new derailleur, it may not be worth the effort.

If you decide to buy a touring bike, be sure it has three chainrings and a large rear cog of at least 24 teeth (more is better).

Cyclometers

A cycle computer is very valuable on tour. All of them will calculate your current and average speed and the distance you have gone. You will use both of these functions to help plan your day and navigate as you tour. Most computers calculate your total distance and also let you restart a second odometer that you can use for daily mileage or any other distance that will make things easier for you. You can buy a computer for twenty-five dollars or so and it is worth every penny. You can install it yourself using the printed instructions. There are computers that do everything but fix your flats and of course you can spend a lot of money on some of these. I have one that calculates altitude which has been helpful from time to time, but most of the time what I use are the speed and distance functions.

Aero Bars

You might want to consider aero bars if you have trouble with numbness in your hands. The aero position puts the weight of your upper body on your elbows giving your hands a rest. Aero bars are designed for speed as the very low position greatly reduces air resistance. This is also very helpful for riding into a head wind. However, it is harder to control the bike from the aero position so you should practice without packs until you feel confident. It will also make it more difficult to use some handlebar bags.

Mirrors, Lights, and Fenders

You should carry a flasher for the rear and a white light for the front of your bike for night and low visibility conditions. Sometimes people walking or on bikes do not realize how hard it is for motorists to see them unless they are lit up in some way. Reflectors are a good idea as are reflective clothes but you should still have lights.

Along the same lines, you may want to consider a mirror for your bike. I find that the ones mounted on the bike tend to wobble around and are harder to see out of. The ones that attach to your helmet or eyeglasses vibrate at the same rate as your eyes, so I think they are easier to use.

Many touring cyclists use fenders to keep water on the road from splashing too much. They are very effective, but not necessary. Using them or leaving them home is a matter of personal preference. They are most valuable on a tour where you expect a lot of rain or mud.

Where to Shop for a New Bicycle

When you are ready to buy a bike for touring, there are quite a few features to look for. There are many advantages to buying your new machine in a bike shop, rather than a catalog or a department store. You are more likely to deal with salespeople who know which bicycles will meet your needs and be able to answer your questions. They will also help you get the right size frame and adjust it correctly. The same people will do any repairs or re-adjusting that you need in the future and they will already be familiar with you and with the bike. You will also be better able to negotiate with a bike shop about different options you may want. With a department store bicycle, what you see is what you get. A bike shop will be willing to upgrade and add or remove options to suit your needs.

You should try riding several bikes to feel the differences in handling and comfort. If the shop is not willing to let you take a few bikes out for a spin, go somewhere else.

Consider used bikes as well, but be careful. You do not want a bike that has been in a crash and was put back together badly. Let an expert check it out before you buy.

Frame Materials

You will find bike frames made out of steel alloys, aluminum, carbon fiber composites or titanium. There are excellent quality frames made from each of these.

Steel

Steel is the most commonly used material. People have been using steel for hundreds of years and have figured out ways to blend alloys that are suitable for many different uses. Steel is also strong, easy to work with, and cheap. As a result, you will find the cheapest bikes as well as some of the most expensive, made from steel. Steel is generally heavier than other materials.

Aluminum

Aluminum is popular because it is light and inexpensive. It also does not rust. Most mountain bikes are aluminum and many touring, racing and road bikes are as well. As with steel, design, quality, and price vary. Be sure an aluminum frame is beefed up enough to handle the weight of a rider plus full packs.

Carbon Fiber

Carbon fiber (composite materials) is a poor choice for a touring bike because it is damaged so easily. When you travel with and on your bike, it will get knocked around and a damaged frame may be unsafe.

Titanium

Titanium is the newest frame material. It is light, strong, and flexible. It is not necessary to paint titanium so you do not have to worry about scratches or chips. The only two disadvantages I know of are high price and limited design. While titanium is gaining popularity quickly for racing bicycles, I have not yet seen titanium used for a touring bicycle.

Strength and Weight

You will be carrying a lot of weight, so strength is important. The easiest way to increase strength is to add metal, which means that many touring bikes are relatively heavy. In the grand scheme of things, a pound or two makes relatively little difference on a fully loaded touring bike.

Frame Geometry

Frame geometry is also important. This refers to the angles formed when the tubes are joined. A good touring bike is almost like a racing bike that has been pulled by its wheels and stretched from front to back. Thus the wheels are further away from each other. This is referred to as a long wheel base. A long wheel base builds more flex into the bike, which makes it more absorbent of road bumps and vibrations. It is not always easy to tell these angles and distances by just looking at them. Ask the salesperson the wheel bases and tube angles of several bikes in the store to get an idea of which ones will be the best.

Mountain bikes are designed to be strong, however, they are meant to carry weight in the middle (the rider) and not extra weight over the wheels. They are also not necessarily designed for comfort.

Hybrid bicycles combine various components of both mountain bikes and road bikes, hence the name. The wheels are the same size as road bikes, but are wide like an mountain bike. They have straight handlebars combined with frame geometry more like a road bike. They are sturdier than road bikes and tend to be more comfortable than mountain bikes. They are adequate for touring and Michael rides one on most of our tours. But if you are looking for a touring bike, bypass hybrids and go for one more specifically designed for that purpose.

Bicycles Designed for Women

Most bicycles are designed for the "average" man. Anyone who is very different from this model person may find it hard to locate a bike that fits well. For a while, there was a theory that women have proportionally longer legs and shorter torsos than men. The statistics have not supported this theory, however, it is still true that many women are more comfortable on bikes with shorter top tubes than the norm. Also, women as a group are shorter than men as a group and it is sometimes difficult to find a frame small enough for a short woman. There are several ways to cope with these issues.

With twenty-six inch wheels, designers can make the entire frame proportionally smaller without changing the basic frame geometry.

On a gravel road, such as this beautiful one in Cape Breton, Nova Scotia, a hybrid bike with not-too-skinny tires is best.

Even though 700 C (or 27-inch) wheels limit the reduction of the size of the frame, the frame geometry can be altered to make the bike smaller. One designer, Georgina Terry, puts a smaller wheel on the front and uses the standard 700 C on the back. Once again, the frame geometry is adjusted.

Mountain bikes and Mixte and lowered-top-tube bikes are often more comfortable for women and other shorter riders than standard road and hybrid bikes. Mixtes have twin lateral tubes running from the top of the steering tube to the rear axle, crossing the seat tube at an intermediate point, while lowered-top-tube designs achieve the same low instep with a single tube from the top of the steering tube to a point halfway down the seat tube. They are also called "step-through" frames. Smaller riders can straddle these bikes more easily than standard designs.

Folding Bikes

Folding bikes have come a long way over the last decade. There are still technical problems to be worked out, like cables that are so long that they tend to kink easily. But there are quite a few good quality folding bikes for touring. While they are still too expensive for me, I have my eye on them for future consideration. They certainly solve many of the problems of transporting a bicycle. Some of them are sold with a packing case. One of the Bike Friday models available comes with a case that can also be used as a trailer. If you look at these, keep in mind that not all of them are designed for touring.

Recumbent Bicycles

Recumbent bikes are enjoying a growth in popularity. The recumbent position is more comfortable for some people, especially those with back problems. It is also easier on the neck and the hands.

It takes very different muscles to pedal a recumbent, so be sure you have lots of practice before you tour on one. If you decide to try touring by recumbent, you will have fewer pack options, so you will need to pack carefully and possibly give some thought to pulling a trailer. As the number of recumbents increases, expect to see an increase in available accessories, including touring packs.

Cargo Trailers

While we are on the subject, lets talk about cargo trailers even though they are not part of the bicycle. Trailers are becoming more popular and are now available in several models and styles. Some cyclists use trailers instead of panniers and some use them in addition to them.

People on tandems as well as recumbents sometimes find that they cannot load all of their gear on only two wheels and need the extra cargo space the trailer provides. Most tandem riders find that pulling the trailer is barely noticeable with two people to share the load.

People traveling with children often need more gear, and young children are not strong enough to carry their own. This means Mom and Dad have to carry more gear and a trailer may be just what is needed. While the extra effort is significant, the arrangement in general seems to work out well in most cases.

One advantage of a trailer is that the bicycle handles more like an unloaded bike. It is not as clumsy as a bike with full packs. However, trailers can interfere with the way the bike tracks. Some people find that it is more difficult to handle a bicycle pulling a trailer than a bike loaded with full packs. This varies from one trailer model to another as well as from one cyclist to another. Trailers that keep the weight low and have a shorter distance between the wheels seem to track better.

Everyone agrees that you must follow the weight and space limitations the manufacturer recommends. Overloading will cause the trailer to be much more difficult to handle.

Trailers attach to the seatpost, the bike frame, or the wheel hub. The ones that attach to the seatpost or frame seem to get higher marks from cyclotourists.

Braze-Ons

Once you have chosen the basic design for your new bike, look at the details. Look for eyelets and braze-ons that allow you to attach various extras to the frame. Most bikes have at least two sets of screw-holes for attaching water bottle cages. Many designed for touring will have three. This is a nice touch.

There should also be places to attach both front and rear panniers. There may be other attachments for lights and other niceties, but these are the most important. Be sure to have the salesperson give you a "tour" if you see holes or hooks that you do not recognize.

Gears Again

We have already discussed gears: get a bike with three chainrings and a cassette with large cogs in the rear (at least 24 teeth, the more the merrier). Most of the smallest (hardest) of the rear cogs are about the same from bike to bike.

Gear Shifters

You will find gear shifters in a couple of places. The older style is to have them on the down tube. Many new bikes locate them inside of the brake levers. This is much preferable to the lower position. Shifters on the ends of the handlebars (bar-end shifters) are making a come-back. To me, these make the most sense for touring. Having small hands, I find it is a bit too far of a reach for the brake levers shifters. They can also interfere with the handlebar bag.

On straight handlebars, usually the shifters are grips on the end of the bars that turn or push buttons. I prefer the push buttons.

Flat tires are a way of life for cyclists. Be prepared to deal with them.

Handlebars

I prefer drop handlebars. They give you more hand positions so you can avoid pressing on the same nerves all day long. They are also very helpful in head winds. You have more control with drop bars. However, straight handlebars are easier on the back for some folks who find the lower position uncomfortable. Again, you can find excellent touring bikes with either.

Brakes

All cable brakes operate by the same basic mechanism. When you squeeze the brake lever, the brake cable is pulled toward the lever. This squeezes the brake arms together and pushes the pads against the rim. You will need more strength to stop a fully loaded touring bicycle. Modern touring bikes are equipped either with Cantilever brakes or with direct-pull, or V-brakes. On these models, the brake arms are mounted to the bike's frame on opposite sides, whereas on conventional brakes, the brake arms are mounted together at a single point, and they are less powerful. As a general rule, cheap bikes have cheap brakes.

Wheels

All other factors being equal, a smaller wheel is stronger than a larger one. Once again, design makes a large difference. You can find high quality 700 C wheels that are stronger than cheap twenty-six inch wheels.

One advantage of 26-inch wheels is that you can find inner tubes in more places than for 700 C tires. You can buy them in any department store that sells kids bikes. This can be handy on the road but make sure the tube has the correct valve.

For those of us who are shorter than average, 700 C wheels may be too big and you may get a better fit with twenty-six inch wheels. However, you will find excellent touring bikes with both sizes and strong proponents of each.

But don't wait for that dream bike: Start touring with the bike you are riding now. You can upgrade and reconfigure as you get more experience. The important thing is to go.

7.

Road Repairs

IN this chapter, I will cover a few basic repairs that I think a touring cyclist should know and the tools needed for them. They are all easy to perform and require only a few tools.

I consider these to be the minimum skills needed. If you plan to travel to remote areas where it may not be possible to get assistance for many days, you will need to know more. If you are not confident in your repair skills, bring a small book on emergency repairs with you on your tour.

For each repair, I have underlined the tools needed. More information on tools is at the end of this chapter.

Saddle Height

Adjusting the saddle height is very easy. Your saddle is on a post that goes into the frame of the bike. (Figure 7.1) At the place on the frame where the post goes in, there is a bolt or a quick-release lever which can be loosened to adjust the seat height. Most likely you will need an Allen wrench, although some older bikes may require a box wrench or an adjustable wrench. Don't forget to tighten it up again.

Saddle Angle

There are bolts on the top of the seatpost that will allow you to change the saddle angle. You will need an Allen wrench, adjustable wrench or a box wrench. Tip the horn down to try to make an uncomfortable saddle easier on your tush. Tip the horn up if you feel like you are sliding down onto the handlebars.

The same bolt allows you to move the seat farther forward or backward. Try different positions and go with the most comfortable.

Handlebars

You can raise or lower the handlebars in much the same way as you adjusted the seat height. The handlebars are attached to the stem, which goes into the frame at the front tube. (Figure 7.2)

The stem is held in at the top, usually with an Allen bolt. Loosen this bolt with an Allen wrench, but do not raise it more than a half inch. The stem is made in two pieces. When you tighten it, the two pieces are pulled together, which wedges the stem inside the fork. To loosen them and adjust the handlebar height or to take the stem out, you may need to give the top a good whack. A rubber mallet is a good choice, but any hard tool wrapped in a cloth will do. Obviously, you do not want a rubber mallet weighing you down on the road, so improvise on your tour.

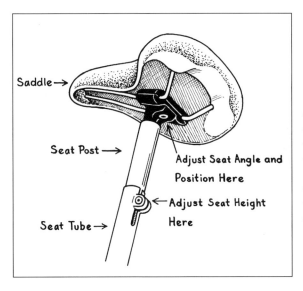

Saddle →

Seat Post →

Adjust Seat Angle and Position Here

Seat Tube →

←Adjust Seat Height Here

Fig. 7.1.
Adjusting your saddle is easily achieved by loosening one of two bolts. The one under the saddle adjusts the angle and relative forward position of the saddle. The one on the seat lug (just behind the top of the seat tube) adjusts the height.

Be sure you do not raise the handlebars too high. The lower piece of the stem should never be visible.

Truing a Wheel

You will need to be able to spin the wheel to true it. On the road, the easiest way to do this is to turn the bike upside down. Watch the wheel as it turns and note where it rubs or wobbles.

You will notice that the spokes alternate. For instance, on the rear wheel, every other spoke attaches to the center of the wheel on the side of the hub where your gears are. The other spokes attach to the side without the gears. (Figure 7.3)

Think of the spokes as pulling the rim. They pull the rim to the side of the hub where they attach. That is, the spokes on the side where the gears are located pull the rim toward the gears and vice versa.

To pull the rim back in line, locate the spokes that are the closest to the spot that rubs. You will have to loosen the spoke that is on the side that rubs and tighten the other side. You will need a spoke wrench or a small adjustable wrench. Turn the nipple, which is on the rim where the

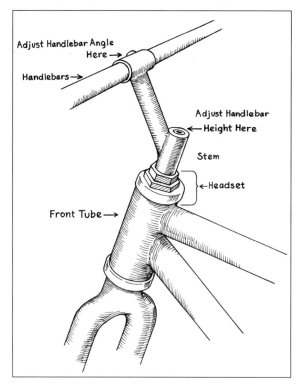

Adjust Handlebar Angle Here →

Handlebars →

Adjust Handlebar Height Here →

Stem

← Headset

Front Tube →

Fig. 7.2.
You can adjust the handlebars easily as well. Loosening a bolt allows you to adjust the height or the angle.

spoke inserts. (Figure 7.4) This is squared off and your wrench can grip it. To tighten the spoke, turn the nipple clockwise as you look at it through the rim. Counter clockwise will loosen it. You may need to turn the nipple several times. Keep spinning the wheel each time you make an adjustment and continue until the wheel is spinning without wobbling. You may need to loosen or tighten a couple of spokes on either side as well.

Replacing Spokes

Spokes almost always break at the head, where they attach to the hub. Remove the broken spoke whether or not you are going to replace it now. Unscrew the broken spoke from the rim and wiggle it out of the other spokes.

If you do not have a spare or do not want to take the time right away to replace the broken spoke, loosen the two spokes on either side of the one that broke until the wheel spins freely.

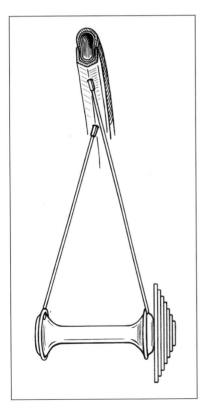

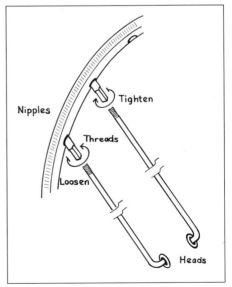

Left: Fig. 7.3. Spokes alternate from one side of the hub to the other, as shown on the left.
Below: Fig. 7.4. Looking through the rim, tighten spokes by turning clockwise and loosen by turning counterclockwise

If you break a spoke on the rear wheel on the same side as the gears, you will need to remove the gears to replace the spoke. If you do not have the special tool to do this, you will have to true the wheel as best you can and have the spoke replaced at a shop.

When you are ready to replace the spoke, turn the bike upside down again. One end of the spoke has a head on it. (Figure 7.4) This is the end that will attach to the hub. There are holes on the hub. Lace the spoke through the hole and place it so that it is on the same side in the same orientation as the broken one. Screw the nipple onto the spoke. When the spoke is in place, true the wheel as we have already discussed.

It is a good idea to carry at least one extra spoke. A regular spoke is long and pointy, which is a nuisance to carry in your pack. Instead, tape your spares onto the inside of one of the chainstays. Michael and I also carry a Kevlar spoke. These are threads of Kevlar, a strong flexible plastic, that you lace onto the hub and screw the nipple on in much the same way as a conventional spoke. They are light and take up very little room in your tool kit. They are not as strong, however, and you should replace it with a regular spoke as soon as you can.

Fixing a Flat

First, you will need to remove the wheel. If your bike has quick-release wheels, you will not need any tools. A skewer goes through the middle of the hub and there is a lever on one side and a thumb nut on the other. The thumb nut screws onto the skewer, which tightens the wheel onto the dropouts. To remove the wheel, flip the lever which will loosen it. Next, unscrew the skewer by holding the thumb nut and turning the lever counterclockwise until it can clear the end of the dropouts (especially on a front wheel, which is often equipped with prongs or some other device to prevent accidental wheel removal). You may need to whack downward on the top of the wheel with your hand to get it out of the dropouts, where the wheel attaches to the frame.

You may also need to release your brakes. Not all brakes have quick-releases but check yours for an easy way to loosen the pressure on the brake arms by loosening the cable. It will be close to the brake arms and would involve slipping the cable off or out of a holder of some kind or it may be a small lever or switch. If you cannot find one, do not worry about it. But next time you are near a bike shop stop in and ask someone if they can find one. It makes taking the wheels off and putting them on much easier.

If you do not have quick-release wheels you will need a wrench that fits the nut on the hub. Loosen the nut, remove the washer if there is one, and remove the wheel. There may be more than one washer. Remember the order you removed them in so you can replace them correctly. Bicycles that do not have quick-release are not likely to have quick-release brakes so you will have to put some pressure on the wheel to get it on and off.

You will need tire levers. You can buy a set of three plastic levers for a couple of bucks. They are small and lightweight. Many of the bicycle multi-tools include levers. You insert the flat end of the lever under the rim of the tire. Pry the rim off and hook the other end of the lever on a spoke. (See Figure 7.5) Place a second lever a few inches away from the first. Do the same with the third. When you have inserted all three levers under the rim, you will be able to pull the whole tire off the rim by hand with ease.

The valve on the inner tube sticks out through the rim. Presta valves have a nut to hold them in place that you need to remove. Push the valve through the rim and remove the inner tube.

Now you need to take out your pump. There are several kinds including some that will attach directly to your bike frame. There are others that are small enough to fit inside your pack. I have one that is so small it fits into my under-the-saddle bag. Be sure that your inner tube and pump are compatible, that is, if your inner tube has a Presta valve, your pump should fit a Presta valve. Use your pump to inflate the inner tube to find the hole.

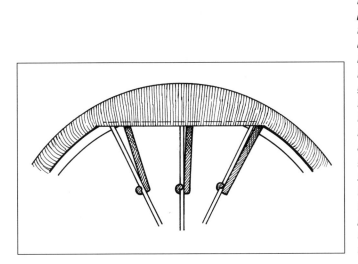

Fig. 7.5. Use tire levers to pry the tire off the rim. They usually come is a pack of three. When you get the first one under the tire, wedge it on a spoke to anchor it while you insert the second one. By the time the third one is in place, the tire will come off easily.

If your tire went flat as you bounced up or down a curb or pot hole, or hit something, you may have a "snake bite," also called a pinch flat. These are two tiny slits right next to each other. Usually, they are close enough to be covered by one patch. Be sure to look for a second hole any time you fix a flat. It is a drag to repair the tube, put the tire back on, blow up the tire and put the wheel on only to have the tire go flat again right away.

For the same reason, check the inside of the tire carefully. Whatever punctured the tube may still be lurking in there and you want to remove it completely. It could be a splinter of glass, a wire from the tire or some other sharp object, so be careful as you search for it.

When you have located the hole, use the sandpaper supplied in the patch kit to rough up the area where the hole is. This will allow the patch to adhere. If you are using glueless patches, remove the backing on the patch and place it on the hole. Rub hard over the entire patch.

While they are quicker and easier, glueless patches are not as strong as those with glue. They are fine in most situations but for larger holes, especially on the weight-bearing rear wheel, you should consider conventional glued patches. For these, you must put the glue on the hole and rub it around so that the area of the glue is larger than the patch. The glue must dry before you put the patch on. It will not seal if the glue is wet. This usually takes about five minutes. Then remove the paper backing and apply the patch. Again, rub it on well.

Insert the patched tube between the tire and rim. Be careful not to pinch the tube. It must be completely inside the tire. It also must not be twisted. Some people recommend pumping up the tube just a little to help place it in the tire smoothly. Insert the valve through the rim. If it's a Presta, attach the nut. Pull the tire on with your hands if possible. You can use the plastic levers for a little help, but do not use screwdrivers or anything else that could damage the tire, inner tube or wheel rim. When you have it all back together, pump the tire up. I need to put my wheel on with a deflated tire because inflated it will not clear the brakes, and I do not have quick-release brakes. If this is the case for you, you should still pump the tire up before you put it on the bike to make sure your patch is holding. Then let the air out, put the wheel on, and pump up the tire again. Oh, come on! It's not *that* much work.

Some holes are just too darned big for a patch to hold. Always carry a new spare inner tube or two with you on your tour, just in case.

You may want to consider a foldable tire, as well, although I have never traveled with one. In Italy, Michael slashed the side of his tire and sewed it up with heavy-duty thread and an embroidery needle. Holes in tires can also be fixed on the road by putting a "boot" on the inside of the tire. Plastic food wrappers, duct tape or a piece of heavy cloth can all be used as a jury-rig to get you to the next bike shop.

Brakes

Brakes can be adjusted very easily with no tools. There is a little thumb screw, called an adjustment barrel, at the end of the brake cable closest to the brakes. To adjust the brakes so that the pads will be fully pressed with less squeezing, tighten the screw (turn clockwise). To adjust them so that the pads will not be fully pressed so quickly, loosen the screw (turn counter-clockwise). (Figure 7.6)

Brake Pads

Adjust the brake pads if they are not centered on the rim. Use a small adjustable wrench to loosen the nut that holds the pads on, move the pads, and then tighten the nut again.

Adjusting the Derailleurs

Each time you shift, the gear cable either tightens or loosens. This pulls the derailleur in or lets it out, taking the chain with it. Your derailleur

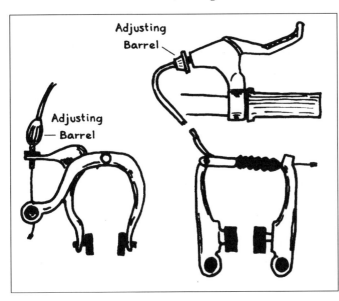

Fig. 7.6.
You can loosen
or tighten your
brakes using
an adjusting
barrel. It is
located on the
brake cable,
either next to
the brake or
next to the
brake lever.

has a barrel adjuster similar to the brakes. There is one right next to the derailleur and on many bikes there is one at the shifter or close to it. If your derailleur is rattling when you are not shifting, the derailleur is not in exact alignment with the gears.

Flip the bike upside down. You will need to look at the derailleur straight-on from the back. You will also need to shift gears and turn the cranks. This is much easier if you have a helper to shift and pedal. As the derailleur moves, notice which gears are out of alignment and in which direction. Turn the barrel adjuster until the everything lines up. This procedure is followed for both front and rear derailleurs.

The barrel adjuster near the shifter allows you to adjust the derailleur while you are riding. Obviously, you cannot see the alignment, but you can hear the rattle. Just keep turning until the noise goes away.

Crank Arm

If the pedal mechanism feels loose, it could be caused by three things the crank arm is loose, the pedal bearings are loose, or there is a problem with the bottom bracket. The easiest to fix is a loose crank arm. Remove the dust cover and use a socket wrench or Allen wrench to tighten it. (Figure 7.7)

The pedal bearings are a pain in the neck to get at and adjust. The bottom bracket requires a special tool whether you have sealed bearings or the old ball and race style. For the old style, you can adjust the bottom bracket yourself if you have the right tool. Some cyclists prefer these

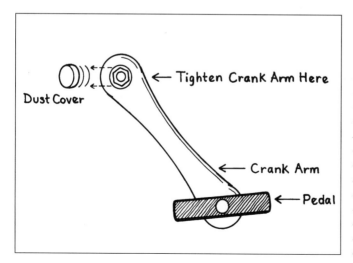

Dust Cover

← Tighten Crank Arm Here

← Crank Arm

← Pedal

Fig. 7.7.
If one of the crank arms is loose, remove the dust cover and use a socket wrench or an Allen wrench (depending on the type of bolt) to tighten the bolt that holds the crank to the bottom bracket.

because they can fix them anywhere in the world. Racers like them because they have lower friction. But they are also more likely to loosen. On the other hand, sealed bottom brackets cannot be adjusted. They have to be replaced. If the problem is not a loose crank arm, take the bike to a mechanic. You will want to be sure this is not a problem before you start your tour.

Tools You'll Need

Bicycles are put together with a bunch of different nuts, bolts, and screws. You should bring tools that will allow you to tighten, loosen, and otherwise modify them.

The tools you might need include the following:

◻ Allen or Hex wrenches that will fit your
seatpost
saddle
handlebars
stem bolt
crank arm
water bottle braze-ons
racks
brakes
brake pads and
any other Allen bolts you see on your bicycle. A number of these
will take the same wrench.

◻ Box wrenches that will fit any of the above that use hex bolts instead of Allen bolts

◻ Spoke wrench to fit your spokes

◻ Socket wrench to fit
1. wheel hub if you do not have quick-release wheels
2. crank arm if it is not an Allen bolt

◻ Small adjustable wrench to use on pedals and any of the above as necessary

◻ A small pair of pliers will also help with the above

◻ Spare spokes, conventional or Kevlar

◻ One or two new spare inner tubes

- Tire levers to remove the tire

- Patches, glueless patches or kit with patches and glue. Be sure the glue has not evaporated

- Pump with the correct attachment for your valves

- Bicycle multi-tool. There are many out there that will include many of these tools in one small package.

- A flathead screwdriver and a Phillips head screwdriver. These will also be included in most bicycle multi-tools and many utility knives also have them.

- A few latex surgical gloves will keep your hands clean when you work on the bike.

- Petroleum jelly is an excellent grease remover.

- Sealable container of lubricant. Put this into plastic bags to keep it from making a mess.

- It is also a good idea to bring along a couple of nuts and bolts that could substitute if you should lose one along the way. This is an especially good idea for your rack.

We have not talked about chain tools, which are also included in most bicycle multi-tools. If you continue to tour, you will want to learn how to use them, however, the chances of having a problem with your chain are slim so I will not discuss them. Michael and I also carry a crank extractor and a cassette remover specific for our bikes, but I do not think they are absolutely necessary. If you know how to use them, bring them. If not, do not worry about it.

Final Note:

There is very little in the world that you cannot jury-rig to get you to the next town if you have duct (cloth) tape, baling (very thin) wire, a Phillips head and a flat head screwdriver, and a pair of pliers. And you can quote me on that.

8

Clothing

IN this chapter, I am going to tell you everything I can think of that may be helpful to you as you pack your clothing. This will include not only my own experience but what I have learned from other cyclotourists through conversation and reading.

There is very little in this chapter that is absolutely essential, and what is important to one person may be superfluous to someone else. Some people are willing to put up with extra weight and bulk to make sure they have everything they might want. Others wear shorts, shoes, socks, and jersey and carry a jacket and a credit card, while everything else stays home. Your own preferences will determine your final choices.

You do not need specialized clothing. Clothes designed for bicycling frequently have advantages, and the more time you spend in the saddle the more you will appreciate them. However, with a bit of advice, you can adapt what is already in your closet. Then as you gain experience and learn what works or doesn't work for you, you can begin to collect bicycling clothes. Your preferences will dictate which items you buy first. You may find that you never feel a need for one item or another. Going on a spending spree right away may be just a waste of time and money.

Bring clothing that you have worn several times. Discover and correct any problems before you start your tour.

The Case for Helmets

Wear a helmet. When I started touring, lo, these many years ago, none of us wore helmets. But that was not a good idea.

A few years ago, I hit an open sewer drain on my daily commute. The front wheel dropped in and the frame hit on the down tube and it cracked. My wheel "tacoed" (visualize a wheel in the shape of a taco shell) and I landed on the asphalt face first. My chin was ripped off my jaw bone, leaving a three-inch gash inside my mouth. A small artery was cut, I broke a tooth and my face was purple and swollen from my eyebrows down. Amazingly, the brunt of the fall was actually to my forehead. My helmet cracked, but there was no damage to my head above the helmet line. If I had not been wearing a helmet, it would have been my skull that cracked.

Safety First

Virtually all helmets manufactured today meet or exceed the standards of either the Snell Foundation or the ANSI or both. This means that all new helmets are equally safe. More expensive helmets may be lighter, more comfortable, more aerodynamic or have better ventilation. The price may also reflect style and name-brand status, but you can be assured that any new helmet with Snell or ANSI approval is safe.

The same is not true of used helmets, however. The styrofoam shell degrades with time, even if it is not worn. Replace yours every five years or so and do not buy used helmets. Replace it if you take a fall or if the helmet is hit hard in some other way. It is not always possible to see that it is structurally damaged, so assume it is and throw it away even if it looks OK. Pinching pennies on style or comfort is fine, but do not take chances with your precious noggin.

Synthetic Versus Natural Fibers

Synthetic materials, such as polypropylene, polyester, nylon, rayon, and spandex are the most common choices for bicycling clothes. Synthetic fibers do not absorb water as cotton does. They dry quickly and do not hold moisture against your skin. This is important for several reasons.

Laundry is easier on the road for cycling and non-cycling clothing made of synthetics. Cotton T-shirts dry more slowly, and you are more likely to be a pedaling clothesline the next day.

Non-absorbency makes bike clothing more comfortable and even safer under some circumstances. Moist skin is softer than dry skin, and it is easier for chafe and blisters to be a problem. Non-absorbent clothing will allow your sweat to evaporate faster, and therefore your skin will stay drier.

On cool rainy days, you will stay warmer in materials that do not absorb water because they do not loose the their ability to insulate, unlike cotton.

Having said that, I have worn cotton T-shirts on many tours and they were fine. I always made sure I did not wash all my shirts at the same time so at least one would be dry the next day and I was always careful to have warm dry clothes to put on at the end of a rainy day. Also, lightweight, light-colored, loose-fitting cotton clothing is sometimes the most comfortable on a hot day.

Gloves

Gloves should be among the first items you buy. Any glove will prevent blisters. Those designed for biking have padding in the palm where you are most likely to press on the handlebars. This helps avoid irritating the nerves in your hand from hours of pressure on the same spot.

Also, if you take a minor fall, you are likely to put your hands out in front of you instinctively. The gloves will prevent scraping up the skin on your hands.

You can buy many different types of cycling gloves that range from a few dollars to ridiculously expensive. You should have a fingerless pair for warm weather and a full-fingered (not full-figured) pair for cooler conditions. Some people use regular gloves, especially in cold weather, which is fine providing they are comfortable.

I do not have waterproof gloves, and sometimes I end up putting on soggy gloves the day after a rain. However, I do not consider this much of a problem. You may disagree. If so, bring along two pairs of gloves, or perhaps a pair made out of water-resistant, but breathable material. If the material does not allow some of your sweat to dissipate, your hands will be wetter from sweat than they would have been with no gloves at all.

We also carry latex surgical gloves to keep our hands clean when working on the bike.

Chafing Problems

Chafe is the enemy. You need chafe protection any place where your skin rubs against the bike, especially if there is likely to be sweat as well. Don't let chafing continue. You may get through the day, but the next day you will be miserable. Stop for a few minutes, find out what is causing it, and eliminate the problem.

Cycling Shorts

Your derriere and inner thighs are the most likely places to be violated by chafe. For this reason, your choice of pants is very important.

Cycling shorts and tights definitely have an advantage over other shorts and pants. Many people find that cycling shorts are their first purchase of specialized clothing. The elasticized, longer legs keep your thighs from rubbing on the saddle. The seam construction and the chamois pad prevent chafe to all those delicate areas that contact the saddle. While the chamois is a pad, it is not really intended as padding. It is for adsorption of sweat, which also reduces chafe.

Cycling shorts are meant to be worn next to the skin, without underwear. The underwear will put you right back into clothing that binds, chafes, and keeps your sweat next to your skin. This is why most of us carry at least two pair of shorts. You can wear one pair during the day, wash it out at night, and have another pair to put on if the first is not yet dry.

I wear cycling shorts now but I resisted them for a long time for reasons of personal vanity. (Me? Out in public in spandex? No thanks.) If you are not yet ready for spandex, try walking length shorts. Synthetic materials are better than cotton or canvas, for the reasons we have already discussed. An elastic waistband makes the hunched over cycling position more comfortable. The longer the legs, the better they will protect. However, loose legs ride up which will leave your skin vulnerable to chafe.

Consider wearing cycling liners. They are cheaper than cycling shorts and may be a good compromise for your first tour. Some of these have a modified chamois and most have non-chafing seams. Even those without a chamois pad will be more comfortable than walking shorts because the elasticized legs will stay down and protect your thighs. They come in different sizes in either white or black and are sold in most bike shops.

Cycling Shoes

Shoes are probably the most difficult clothing choice that a cyclotourist faces. I bought cycling shoes very early in my touring career. I think the bones in my feet came from the spare parts department because they seem to be made for three of four completely different individuals. It does not take much to make them cranky. On the other hand, Michael (who was told by one sports podiatrist that he had the most technically perfect feet he had ever seen) continued to ride with sneakers until we switched to cleats (clipless pedals), which require special shoes. It is more important with shoes than any other article of clothing that you ride many times with the pair of shoes you intend to take on the tour.

There are many pieces of equipment and gear that I economize on. (Sure that $70 jersey is pretty, but is it worth the extra $40?) But I never compromise on shoes or saddles. Get it on sale if you can, but do not buy it if it is not comfortable.

If you ride without toeclips or cleats your choice of shoe will be less important. You can move your foot around on the pedal and this change of position will help prevent any one part of your foot from bearing all of the load. toeclips allow a little change in position. With cleats, your foot movement is further reduced and so is the area that your foot is pressing on. This means that a small area of the ball of the

Why is this man smiling? Because a little rain can't darken a sunny disposition. And a rain jacket helps, too.

foot takes on all of the force of pedaling.

However, toeclips and cleats make pedaling much more efficient by allowing you to use both the downstroke and the upstroke of the pedaling motion. You will tire less quickly and climbing hills is much easier. The cleats are adjustable to a limited degree which helps. I have mine as far back as possible to avoid putting too much pressure right on the end of the ball of my foot. But there is not a lot of leeway. Some cleats "float," that is they allow a little foot movement when you are clipped in.

Stiff soles spread the pressure to the entire bottom of the foot. You can find cycling shoes with varying amounts of stiffness. The stiffer they are, the easier they are on your feet for pedaling but a very rigid sole is harder to walk in.

There are two basic kinds of cleats. In the one racers use most often, the cleat is attached to the bottom of a thin rigid sole. The cleat is a big lump on the bottom of the shoe. These are not a good choice for touring. The shoes are virtually impossible to walk in, even briefly. I have seen bikers risking their lives walking from the bike to the lunch stop! Some bikers carry a pair of flip-flop sandals in their jersey pocket but I would find it annoying and uncomfortable to have them poking me in the back all day. And I cannot imagine carrying my bike up to the hotel room in flip-flops. A better solution is to stick to the second types of cleats.

Mountain bike cleats are recessed in a thick sole. This means that you can walk more or less normally in them. These are the best ones for touring. They are usually not as stiff as the rigid racing shoes, although they can be found in different amounts of stiffness. I prefer the stiffest mountain bike shoes I can find.

The problem with selecting shoes is that you usually cannot try them on the bike before you buy. The cleats are bought and attached separately (the shop will do this for you if you want, although it is easy to do yourself) so the pair you are considering will not have them. This means you cannot see how your foot will feel when you are pedaling. And yet the shoes are expensive enough that you do not want to make a mistake. Some stores will exchange shoes if you return them within a short time. Ask about this before you buy. For your first set of cleats it is a good idea.

For some reason, bike shoes tend to be narrow, especially through the ball of the foot and the toes. Be sure the shoes you get fit you well. Too much pressure on the forefoot can become very uncomfortable.

The bike shoes I have seen tend to be brightly colored and flashy, making them less acceptable in public off the bike. We continue our search for bike shoes that look like street shoes but I guess those do not advertise the manufacturer as well.

Shoes without laces are great because laces get caught on the chainring. You can always tuck the laces into the top of the shoe, but you have to remember that before you start to ride.

Socks

Choose socks that fit well. Socks that are too big or do not hold their shape may bunch up inside your shoes, causing chafe and blisters. Stretchy materials, such as spandex, improve the fit and keep the shape after many washings.

I always carry at least two pair of socks so that I always have one pair that is clean and dry. I also carry at least one additional pair that I do not use for riding. I hate wet feet, so I keep at least one pair in a plastic bag with other clothes, so that even if I have to ride in the rain all day, I will have a warm, dry pair of socks to put on when we stop.

Sunglasses

Bring a pair of sunglasses with you. Staring into bright light for hours is fatiguing. They will also keep bugs, dust, and wind out of your eyes. Polarized glasses are the most helpful in dealing with bright light. Some people wear yellow lenses in low light because it improves their vision. Wrap-around sunglasses are the best and offer the most protection.

For those of you, like me, who need prescription lenses, there are lots of sports glasses that allow you to use them. I do not use them because the sports lenses do not offer a good enough option for my prescription. I should warn you though that they are very expensive. With my vision, I am used to paying outrageous costs for glasses, but you might not, and I would not want you to faint right there in the office.

Cycling Jerseys

The advantage of specialized cycling jerseys is not as great as with shorts. If you want to save money, you can wear T-shirts. I recommend ones made of a blend of cotton and synthetics rather than all-cotton, for the reasons already given. There are also lots of non-cycling shirts made of synthetics. Simple nylon or polypropylene T-shirts are adequate and you can buy them in sports or discount department stores for a fraction of the cost of a biking jersey.

Cycling jerseys are superior to the T-shirts in a few ways, however. The front zipper allows you to regulate the air flow over your chest. The back is longer to accommodate the hunched over riding position. Since cycling shorts do not have pockets, a rear pocket in the jersey is handy for holding small items you might want while riding, such as a snack, sunscreen, lipgloss or sunglasses.

Jerseys are available with long-sleeves, short-sleeves or no sleeves. You can even get them with zip-off sleeves for even greater versatility. The weight of the material varies from ultra-light for hot weather to pile-lined for cold days.

I tend to buy plain colored jerseys rather than the many brilliantly colored and patterned shirts. First, I do not want to be a pedaling billboard but also, sometimes more discreet clothing can be less intrusive while you are traveling. They are also usually much less expensive than their bold counterparts.

Rain Gear

I always carry a rain jacket that is fairly light and compact and can be worn not only on the bike in the rain, but as a wind jacket and on cool days when you are not riding. If you expect to be cycling in the rain in cool temperatures, consider good quality rain gear. Breathable fabrics are best as you will be much less likely to overheat. We met two women who bicycled from Fairbanks Alaska to San Francisco. They considered their expensive rain gear to be worth every penny.

A rain jacket that is designed for cycling will have a longer back and shorter front designed for the hunched over cycling position. There will also be air vents, sometimes under the arms and frequently under a flap on the back.

I try to avoid cold, wet places when I am on vacation. The one place where we encountered sleet (in August, no less) was Iceland, and, we were not adequately prepared. However, there is usually an option if you use your noodle. I carry extra trash bags on every tour, and sometimes they go on many tours before they are used. But in a pinch, they are waterproof and can be adapted for all kinds of fashionable and functional clothing. On this occasion, we wore large trash bag raincoats and small plastic bag socks. There's always a solution. Wool clothing will keep you warm even after it is wet. Synthetic piles are also excellent choices. They insulate when wet and they are lighter and less bulky than wool.

Usually the most difficult problem with cycling rain gear is that you get too hot. Waterproof materials will also hold your body heat in and at least some of your sweat. Even the so-called breathable fabrics are very warm. This is excellent in cold weather but in more temperate climates, you will roast. I frequently opt for getting wet while I ride, knowing I have a nice dry set of clothes packed in a plastic bag to put on when I stop for the day. I keep my rain jacket in a handy spot to put on whenever I stop for a break or to see the sights. I only carry rain pants when I expect cold, rainy weather.

Ponchos and Capes

Some cyclists carry thin, inexpensive plastic rain ponchos. The advantage to these is that they are light and take up little room. However, they flap around in even the slightest breeze, including the one you are creating just by moving forward through the air. They also do nothing to stop splash-up from the road. Do not bother to bring one unless you are planning on wearing it when you are off the bike.

On the other hand, I have heard wonderful things about capes designed for cycling. They are more contoured than a poncho and are secured better so they do not flap around as much. These seem to be more readily available in Europe than in the U.S. I cannot personally recommend them but other cyclists I have spoken to wax poetic when they are mentioned.

Cold

It is unlikely that a novice cyclotourist will travel to Sweden in January, but no one should limit their options to the tropics, either. I will start this section with suggestions for cool weather and continue to winter cycling clothes for those of you who, like me, continue biking all year. When you start to get chilly, skip to the next section.

Cool or cold weather that is dry is much easier to cope with than cold rain. You will need more layers of clothing. A wind breaker and wind pants are worth bringing on most tours, and they can be worn on cool evenings off the bike. They can also be slipped on over your cycling shorts and shirt when you want to enter some building where spandex would attract too much attention. Remember the warning about shoelaces because it applies to loose-fitting pant legs, too. I have several pairs of sweat pants with little holes on the inside of the right leg from catching on the chainring.

A long-sleeved turtleneck made of synthetic material will come in handy, as will a pair of either loose-fitting, synthetic warm-up pants or spandex tights. For even cooler weather, you may need both. Cycling shops carry them and you can also get them at general sports or department stores. The differences in price are due to several factors. Some are a better quality than others. The material may be thicker or stronger and the seams may be sewn better. Zippers on the bottoms of the legs are very convenient but you will pay quite a bit extra for them. Name brands will cost more, sometimes because of better quality, but not always.

When it gets cold, your feet, hands, and ears are likely to be the first casualties, so keep them warm from the start. Carry long-fingered gloves and possibly ones with insulation. Wool or pile socks are good. There are several kinds of cold weather footwear, some to wear over and some under the shoes. These are designed to shed the wind. They can be expensive and you may want to try putting plastic bags over your feet and then putting your shoes on. Ah! Plastic bags! One of humanity's great inventions.

For your head and ears, consider a pile headband or hat. You will want to wear your helmet as well, so it must be thin. Anything that will keep the wind from shooting through the helmet's vents will help, and the insulation from the helmet will also keep you warmer. Some people find that a nylon covering for the helmet is sufficient. You can buy little ear caps that slip over your ears like a glove. As with everything else, you can spend a lot of money , but you can also use hats and headbands you find in discount stores as long as they fit under your helmet.

The normal riding position encourages wind to funnel down your chest. Turtleneck shirts are adequate for cool temperatures, but you may want a scarf or a neck gaiter for cold weather. A neck gaiter is a ring made of a warm material that you pull over your head. It covers the neck and upper chest and puts a barrier between your chest and the chilly blasts of cold air. The wind is the biggest obstacle to keeping warm on a bike. Wear wind-resistant coverings over as much of your body as possible. This means a hat or helmet cover, something for your face (a bandanna is sufficient in all but the coldest weather), gloves, long-sleeves, long pants, and shoes and socks.

There are many winter clothing items made of down. The advantage of down is that it is light, warm, and very compressible so it does not take up much room. The biggest disadvantage is that, like cotton, it loses all of its ability to insulate if it gets wet. You must be very careful to keep your down items dry. Once again, our old friend the plastic trash bag comes to the rescue. If we are carrying down sleeping bags, we put them into their stuff sacks and then shove the bag into a trash bag and tie the opening. I carried my down vest in a zippered plastic food bag.

Heat

In some ways, excessive heat is more difficult to handle than cold. You can always put on more clothes. Exposing more of your skin will increase the evaporation of sweat, which will help cool you but, you will also increase your chance of sunburn. Some experts have suggested that when sunscreen, which has water in it, evaporates it helps keep you cool.

Loose, light colored clothing is best. Light colors reflect light and heat. Loose clothing will allow air flow which increases the evaporation of sweat.

We have discussed sunglasses. These will help reduce eye strain, which will reduce fatigue in general. A visor on your helmet is also helpful.

The current designs for helmets provide good ventilation through the slots. They are also getting lighter in weight which helps. If you cycle in an area that is frequently very hot, you may want to invest in one of the helmets that are specifically designed for excellent air flow.

Hydration Systems

As long as we are on the subject of the heat, lets talk about "hydration systems." That's a fancy name for specialized water containers. The current favorites are plastic bladders that fit into an insulating, neoprene pouch. This straps onto the middle of your upper back. There is a long tube that acts as a straw so that you can drink easily without moving your hands from the handlebars. People who use these tend to drink more than those who use water bottles attached to the bike frame. This means they are less likely to become dehydrated. However, I hate anything on my back when I ride. There are hydration systems that attach lower on the back, like a fanny pack, and someday I would like to try one of those. Until then, I just keep reminding myself to pick up that water bottle. The hydration systems are expensive but as they become more prevalent and as more companies enter the market, perhaps the price will come down.

Off the Bike

The clothing you bring to wear off the bike depends on the tour. Try to avoid setting up situations where you will need formal clothing. Tuxedos do not travel well squished into a pannier. For respectable but not formal settings, opt for crushable synthetics in pants, shirts, and dresses. Leave your jeans at home. They are heavy and bulky and they are a pain to wash and dry while traveling.

I have a favorite, comfortable sleeveless dress made of rayon. I can wear it sleeveless, with a short-sleeve shirt or a long-sleeve turtle neck depending on the weather. The material has a naturally crinkly quality. So I can always say it's "crinkly" not "wrinkly." Rayon is light, not bulky, and dries quickly after washing. The print, small flowers against black, does not show dirt.

It was hot in Cuba, with some very steep hills, so we took our time and drank frequently.

The good news is that clothing made of synthetics can be found in discount department stores and tend to be less expensive. All right, it is not Armani, but it will do. There is at least one company that makes synthetic fiber, washable, and wrinkle-resistant clothing for men and women. The company is Travel Wise. Telephone and address information is listed in the back of this book. They will send you a free catalog by mail. Clothing made of cotton/synthetic blends are easier to find and are better than all natural fibers.

If you are in a supported tour, you will have room for an extra pair of heavy shoes, while it will not increase the weight you are carrying. For self-contained touring, you want to keep the weight and bulk down. Sandals make a good choice for both men and women. The best choice is a pair of sports sandals made of neoprene soles and nylon straps. They are comfortable, light, and are acceptable in most places. Even my cranky tootsies can endure a whole day of walking in them.

Swimwear is not a problem unless you are planning on bringing scuba gear, so why not bring it, just in case you get the chance to take a dip?

Remember that other people may not be comfortable with folks in tight, revealing biking clothes. Respect the people you are visiting. and have a jacket and pants to pull for "public" appearances.

9.

Packs, Camping Gear, etc.

How Much is Too Much?

I belong to a computer group that discusses bicycle touring. There is a constant debate about how much gear one should bring on a tour. Some people set a rigid weight or space limit and stick to it. Once they arrive at their limit, nothing else goes into the packs. They think carrying more is just a matter of poor planning and too much dependence on "luxuries." Others call those guys wimps who are not strong enough to carry the hundred pounds of gear they haul up mountainsides. I know of cyclotourists carrying camp chairs, small coolers, two-burner stoves with extra propane canisters and many other items most of us would never consider bringing. But the person hauling the stuff around is the only one who matters in deciding what to bring and what to leave home.

When you start to pack, weigh the value of the particular item in terms of comfort, safety, whatever. Then weigh the difficulty of biking up a hill with it in your pack (or even if it will fit in your pack). Each person will come up with a different answer for each piece of gear and each choice will be correct for the person who made it.

Panniers

First of all, you need something to put your gear into. At the very least you should have a rack over your rear wheel and a pair of packs designed for bicycles. The packs are called panniers, pronounced "pan'-yer" or "pan'-ee-er." It comes from the French word panier, which means "basket."

There are other types of packs that we will consider, but rear panniers are the mainstay of touring baggage. You will want to get the largest size you can find and afford. We met a man who was spending a month touring the Pacific coast. He traveled about 75 miles a day, carrying only a handlebar bag. He was wearing all the clothes he brought and carried a few tools, a small camera, a toiletry bag, and a credit card. I salute you if you can be so Spartan, but for most of us, the space fills up quickly and the small packs do not hold enough.

Some people use small panniers so that they will not be tempted to bring too much gear. While taking too much is very easy to do, and you will need to work to avoid it, I think it is much better to get the larger packs, which will give you more options, and exercise self control.

It is hard to find a variety of packs in bike shops but there is a good selection from mail order catalogs and the Internet. Check the reference section for suggestions. Make sure the packs are returnable in case they are not what you expected.

Design Options

There are two basic designs for the main compartment. In one, the top is open like a big sack. The other has a side opening, usually with a rigid frame at the top to keep the bag's shape. Both top and side openings have advantages. The open top packs usually have a larger capacity and will hold both more items and larger gear, like sleeping bags. However, it is hard to strap anything to the rack if the packs are fully loaded. If you want to carry a rack-top pack, sleeping bag or tent on your rack, a rigid frame, side-opening pack may work best for you.

Attaching the Pannier to the Rack

Most of the panniers available are at least adequate, but there are a few features to consider when making your choice. You will be removing the packs frequently during your trip so make sure they are easy to put on and take off. Despite all of the bells and whistles available, I like a simple attachment. A hook or loop on the bottom attaches to the rack near the wheel hub. It is connected to a tight spring or bungee, which is connected to two hooks on the top of the pack. You pull up on the pannier until the top hooks on to the rack. Gadgets made to stabilize the packs or increase tension may just make it hard to use.

Frame Structure

There should be a hard board, frequently made of plastic, inserted into the side that goes next to the bike. This will keep an unloaded or under loaded pack from flapping and getting caught in the spokes. Look for well-constructed seams and sturdy zippers. The bolts or rivets that hold the frame to the pack should be strong. Panniers get knocked around on tour and you want yours to hold up. I prefer bolts over rivets because they can be tightened or replaced if needed.

Pockets Attached to the Main Compartment

Side pockets help keep your gear organized and are convenient for things you want to have readily available. A side pocket that has depth is best; one that is just a flat piece of fabric sewn on the outside of the main compartment will hold very little when the pack is full.

One exception is a pocket made of elasticized material. My packs have one of these, and it is helpful for ID, keys, sunscreen, train tickets or other small items you might want to have close at hand.

Material

Most panniers are made out of cordura, a heavy nylon cloth that has a plastic coating on the inside. Cordura is tough and abrasion-resistant. The plastic lining makes the pack water-resistant, but not waterproof.

There are panniers designed to be waterproof, although I have not used any of these. They are usually made of woven material that is impregnated, rather than just coated, with plastic. The seams are the worst spot for leaking, and in a truly waterproof pack, they should be joined by melting or "welding" the pieces together. Seams that are sewn and coated with a sealant will leak eventually. Most bags advertised as waterproof have a top opening and a large waterproof flap on top.

Even if your pannier is not completely waterproof, you can keep your gear dry with our old friend the plastic trash bag. You can line the entire main compartment with a large bag, or you can use several smaller bags. Be sure to seal the opening either with a zipper-type closing or by tying a knot.

Compression Straps and Bungees

A couple of other nice features are compression straps and loops for attaching straps or bungee cords. Compression straps essentially allow you to decrease the size of the pack when it is not fully loaded. This will keep your pack from flapping and items in the pack from bouncing and shifting.

With straps and bungees, you can secure the pack to the rack better and strap extra items, such as a rain jacket or tent poles, onto the pack or on top of the rack. Straps are also be helpful with attaching gear to the top of the rack. You can also use bungee cords or make your own compression straps.

It's hard to believe all this stuff fits on our bikes, but it does.

Reflective Material

I like to have reflective material on my packs. If the one you buy does not have any, you can use reflective tape or plastic reflectors. Some shops that sell cycling gear have sew-on or adhesive reflective tape or material if your gear has none, or not enough. I try to avoid touring at night, but sometimes it is necessary and I feel much safer knowing cars can easily see me. Reflectors will make cycling safer in any low visibility condition where cars use their headlights, including bad weather.

Shoulder Straps

You should have a shoulder strap for your panniers. If your set does not come with one, buy one at a sports or camping outfitter store. Get a nice, wide one, preferably with padding. There will be someplace on top of the packs where you can strap them together and carry both of them over your shoulder. Place the ends of the shoulder strap as far apart as possible for the most comfortable set-up. If your packs have loops, you can use them. If your packs have no loops for straps, you can use the hand-grip straps in the middle of the top of the pack. This is more awkward but is still better than trying to carry them without a shoulder strap.

Some packs have snaps or some other way of attaching the bags together. This is a great feature.

You can buy rain covers for panniers. I have never used them, but I have heard from everyone I know who has that they are not all they are cracked up to be. They will keep the front of the pack dry, but they funnel the splash-up from the tire directly into the pack. I think it is better to put anything you do not want to get wet into a plastic bag. (You saw that coming, didn't you?)

Handlebar Bags

There is a plethora of other kinds of packs to consider. The next most common type is the handlebar bag. This is very useful for gear you want to remove from the bike every time you leave it even for a few moments. I carry my wallet, passport, and other valuables in my handlebar bag and use it as a vacation pocket book. We customized one of our handlebar bags to carry our camera. You will want to keep your camera handy as you tour. In the handlebar bag, you can shoot your photos while straddling the bike. We can easily carry the camera with us when we see the sights off the bike as well.

Bicycles that have shifters in the brake levers do not carry handlebar bags well. You will need a small bag to fit into the cables without interfering with shifting. I strapped a small bungee around my bag to compress it, but that makes it difficult to get into. This is another advantage to bar-end shifters for touring.

Keep as little weight as possible in handlebar bags because more weight will make steering difficult.

Front Panniers

Small panniers designed to fit on the front are rising in popularity. They usually have a rigid frame and only one compartment. Not only will front packs increase your baggage capacity, but they also help balance the weight on the bike. You will notice the difference most dramatically when you are going down hill. These packs are not necessary and we have toured thousands of miles with only handlebar bags and rear panniers. You can always add them next time or even several years from now.

Front panniers require a rack specifically made for the front wheel. The best racks are the ones that hold the pack as low as possible where it will interfere less with steering. You will need eyelets on the front fork and braze-ons are also helpful.

Rack-Top Packs

Rack-top packs are also becoming more popular, especially for non-touring rides to carry lunch and a jacket. But some people like them for a long tour. They are usually semi-rigid, using foam padding to keep their shape which also keep the bread from getting squished. The foam is insulating and helps keep lunch cool. Once again, do not run out and buy these for your first tour but keep them in mind as you decide what works for you.

Bags of Little Use to the Cyclotourist

There are other packs that I do not find very helpful for touring but I will mention because they are convenient for other kinds of biking. You should never ride without a way to fix a flat and it is a good idea to have a few tools with you as well. With an under-the-seat pack you can carry tools, a patch kit and a spare inner tube. Of course, on tour, you can pack those things in your panniers and will not need the saddle pack.

Frame packs are flat triangles that attach to the top tube and the seat tube. Personally, I think these are silly in any circumstance, but if you get really pressed for cargo space, you might want to consider them. Remember, though, that it will interfere with the normal space for water bottles and a frame pump. But go ahead, I promise not to cluck my tongue or laugh or call you funny names.

I have the same bad attitude about courier bags. I understand why couriers use them. Couriers are making short hops around the city and do not want to be bothered unstrapping stuff and then strapping it on again. But why would you want to balance a shoulder bag hour after hour? Get a rack and get it off your back.

The Right Number of Bags

What if you are rich and do not worry about spending a small fortune on packs and gear? Why not buy all these packs and racks and strap on everything but the kitchen sink?

Carry only what you need to be happy. You have to move all that weight around, and going uphill becomes more difficult by huge leaps as you increase the weight. But also, at some point on your tour, most likely at several points, you will need to move all that gear around off the bike. When you get onto the airplane, when you check into your hotel room, getting on and off the train or bus…, you will need to move all those packs without losing any of them.

This is true even for those on supported tours. It is not likely that there will be a valet or bellhop to haul your gear to and from your room each day. Keep it simple and take as few bags as you can.

Camping

Should you bring camping gear? We almost always do because it gives us more flexibility. However, there are many places where you can get to a hotel or other overnight accommodation every night without difficulty if that is what you want to do. If you don't bring a tent and sleeping bag, you should be conservative in your route planning or at least be aware of alternatives in case there is an unexpected delay.

Sleeping Bags

We have two sets of sleeping bags, a pair of down winter bags, and a pair of synthetic fill summer bags. Because we like each other, we bought bags that zip together. They are also warmer.

The down bags are so light that if we have any doubt about the nighttime temperatures, we can carry them without adding weight. However, down loses all of its ability to keep you warm when it is wet, so you must be careful to keep down bags dry. Are you ready for my continued love affair with plastic bags? Be sure to tie the bag closed.

With sleeping bags filled with synthetic materials, it is not so critical to keep them dry because they can still insulate you from the cold if they are wet. However, trying to sleep in a wet bag would be a very unpleasant way to spend a night. Trash bags are our friends.

Whichever bags we carry, we pack them into compression sacks. These are regular cordura stuff sacks with an extra component. There are straps on the outside of the sack that you tighten to squeeze the bag into as small a space as possible. You cannot store sleeping bags in these because it will permanently compress the fill material, but it is great for travel. They even fit inside our panniers.

Sleeping Pads

The ground can not only be hard, it can be cold, too. A pad under your sleeping bag helps. Foam pads provide insulation as well as padding. In fact, their ability to keep the cold ground from chilling you is better than their ability to cushion your weary bones. Do not bring pads made of open- cell foam, which absorbs water like a sponge. Closed-cell foam does not. Pads that are made of closed-cell foam will say so. If you are in doubt, ask a salesperson.

Some pads have a waterproof exterior shell. Those with a valve to let air in and out are very good.

You can get pads in a variety of sizes and thicknesses depending on your budget and your willingness to haul it around.

Biker Tents

We have a lightweight tent for one to two persons that weighs only three pounds including a rain fly. The top of the tent is made of screen material. This reduces the weight, allows more air-flow (keeping it cooler) and gives us a great view on a clear night. It would be a perfect tent if it were not quite so tiny. It is not a tent that you would want to get stuck in for an extended length of time. On a trip in which we plan to spend more than a couple of days in one campsite and perhaps a considerable amount of time in the tent, we bring our heavier, but taller and wider, two-person half-dome. We met three cyclotourists, each of whom carried their own three to four person tent. Your choice will depend on your standard for comfort and your tolerance for extra weight and space.

Waterproof Tarps

A waterproof ground tarp will assure that rain and moisture from the ground will not seep into the floor of your tent during the night. Tarps are lightweight, take up little room, and are inexpensive. Place the tarp either inside on the floor of your tent or outside on the ground with the tent on top. If you put it underneath, make sure the tarp does not stick out from the side of the tent, or rain will pool on the tarp, making it more likely you will wake up wet. Many ground tarps have a solid color on one side and reflective silver on the other side that reflects heat. lie the tarp silver side up inside the tent in cool or cold weather to keep you warmer.

Table 9-1: Features to consider when buying a camping stove

1. Safety

2. Easy to light and turn off

3. Quality of the burner: consistent flame, easy to adjust, boils water quickly, can be adjusted to a very low setting for simmering

4. Type of fuel used (the more the better)

5. Stability: will your pot sit securely on the burner?

6. Size of fuel tank. Larger tank means longer cooking time before refill, but also larger size and weight

7. Weight and overall size

8. Price

Camp Stoves

We do not always carry a cook stove. On a tour to a warm place where it will be possible to pick up groceries every day, we might leave the stove at home, opting for cooked meals from time to time in restaurants and having meals of ready-to eat food on the go. However, if we plan to camp frequently, we bring our single-burner backpacking stove.

There are numerous models available, any of which are fine for touring. If you decide to buy a stove, consider a multi-fuel one. It is illegal to carry fuel on an airplane so you must buy it at your destination. Having more choices will make it easier to find. We usually buy a quarter's worth of regular gasoline at a service station every several days.

Some fuel is not available everywhere, and consequently stoves that can use many kinds are great. Be sure you have used your stove several times before you start your tour. Work the bugs out ahead of time so that you do not find yourself dining on cold tomato sauce and dry pasta your first night on the road. Also, do not forget to bring a lighter and/or matches with you.

Cooking Gear

A small, nested camping cook kit will contain one or two lightweight pots and a small frying pan. We have a non-stick, six-inch frying pan, a one-pint pot, and a one-quart pot, all made of thin, lightweight stainless

---

Table 9-2: Common camping stove fuels

1. White gas
2. Automobile gasoline
3. Propane
4. Butane
5. Kerosene
6. Diesel
7. Sterno
8. Alcohol

---

steel. You may have something similar in your kitchen cabinets. Think small and lightweight.

Dishes do not fit easily into bike packs so bring as few as possible. A small plastic bowl for each person is sufficient. You can wipe it out between courses. In addition to our water bottles, we bring plastic cups. Coffee or tea sucked out of a sports bottle is just not civilized. Bring a sturdy set of cutlery because cheap plastic will break quickly. The stainless steel sets are lightweight, inexpensive, and much more durable.

Remember to bring cleaning supplies. We use shampoo for all of our jobs requiring soap, and we let our dishes air-dry or toss them into the pack a little damp, but we bring a sponge with a scrubbing pad for washing up pots.

Think about utensils before you go. Will you need a can opener? How about a corkscrew? Bottle opener? Knife? All of those items may be very useful and are included on most utility knives. Michael and I have two Swiss Army knives. Both knives have two blades, can-opener, bottle opener, and flat head screwdriver. Mine also has a small scissors and a corkscrew, while Michael's has a mini-saw and a Phillip's head screwdriver.

Bicycle Computers

A cyclometer is very useful on tour. There are many to choose from but any that give your current speed, average speed, and distance are adequate. Feel free to include whatever technological wonders that amuse or enlighten you. I have one that includes altimeter and thermometer functions. While it has been helpful and entertaining on tours, most of the time I only use the speed and distance functions.

Gadgets and Gizmos

I do not bring cell phones, camcorders, GPS receivers, laptop computers, nuclear reactors, sundials or other technological wonders on my tours. However, some people carry many interesting devices with them. For example, you can keep in contact with others via E-mail if you bring the right equipment. There are even computer programs that will give you an interactive map that updates as you move. These are toys only and are absolutely not necessary. Sometimes they are not even practical, but they can be great fun. Those of you who love these toys know much better than I what you need to consider if you want these with you. So all I will say is, "Have fun!"

Safety

Carry a rear flasher and a white headlight. You can use your headlight as a flash light or vice versa if you choose carefully. We have lights on an elastic band that is worn on the head (a head lamp) as a flashlight and a headlight for the bike. Remember to bring extra batteries.

Reflective clothing is great, and we already discussed reflective tape on packs. Plastic reflectors on pedals and spokes are very effective as well.

I have a bell on my bike, and sometimes I use a mirror attached to my eyeglasses. Some folks have an orange flag flying from the bike or an orange vest with reflective tape. All of these items will make you more visible to traffic.

I have included a small compass in my gear on a couple of occasions when I thought it might be helpful. In remote areas with few landmarks, a compass can be reassuring. Even in urban areas, when you will be turning frequently and it is easy to miss a turn or take a wrong one, the compass can help by telling you if you are going in the right direction.

Locking the Bicycle

Bring a lock. How sturdy will depend on where you are going. It is best to avoid a really heavy lock, but you may want something better than a thin cable. Most likely you will not be able to keep your eye on the bike at every moment so you need insurance that your faithful steed does not leave without you.

Straps and Bungees

I carry an assortment of straps and bungees to hold all of my stuff together. They work out well as a clothesline both on the bike and in your room or campsite.

Photographic Equipment

I enjoy the photographs from my tours and I want a good camera to record as much as possible. We carry a regular 35-mm camera with two lenses that zoom from 28 mm (panoramic) to 210 mm (telephoto) with infinite settings in between. It has automatic options but can also be set manually with more bells and whistles than we will ever use. However, we do use many features that are not available on smaller, lightweight or more fully automatic cameras. If this is not as important to you, there are several very small, light cameras that will stuff into a pocket.

We found that our camera took a beating on tour if we were not careful about how we packed it. Using foam rubber, we padded the inside of one handlebar bag to fit the camera and lenses. There is a little slot for filters and a space for an extra battery. A half dozen rolls of film fit into the pocket on the front of the bag. We can even squeeze in our minipod, a tiny tripod, that we use for timed photos and long exposures.

Plastic Bags and Stuff Sacks

I find it more convenient if I pack my gear into smaller bags and put them into the pannier. I carry a couple of extra stuff sacks, one for dirty clothes and another one or two for food bought along the way.

Stuff sacks are usually made of cordura and are water-resistant. To keep items dry in all conditions, I use (guess what?) plastic bags. Large trash bags are good for sleeping bags and lining the inside of the pannier and there are a variety of smaller food storage bags that will meet many other needs. The best are freezer bags with sealable tops. It is good to carry extra small bags and one or two trash bags. They come in handy in oh so many ways.

We bring either a fanny pack or a day pack to use when we are wandering around off the bike. Almost any fanny pack is fine. Try to find a very lightweight day pack that will squish into a small space.

Toiletry Items

Michael says that hot water is what separates humans from other animals. There is nothing like a nice, hot shower at the end of a long day to soothe the soul, and nothing like one in the morning to wake you up and get the day started right.

We bring a typical compliment of personal cleaning items including shampoo, hairbrush, toothpaste, and toothbrush. We use the shampoo for all of our soap needs from dishes to clothes. We also bring cotton swabs and moisturizer.

I carry a few disposable razors. Michael normally uses an electric shaver and finds it irritating to use razors. He has a battery operated shaver that weighs less than a pound, and the batteries last a few weeks.

If you are camping, you should also bring a partial roll of toilet paper sealed in a zipper plastic bag.

Sunscreen

A bad case of sunburn will slow you down. Bring sunscreen and use it frequently. There is even evidence that evaporation of the water in sunscreen will help keep you cooler than you would be without it. Consider lip gloss with sunscreen and do not forget those sunglasses.

Waking to a view of irises just outside the tent makes camping seem like luxury travel.

Towels

If you are staying in hotels every night, this will not be necessary, however, if you are camping or staying in hostels you need a towel. High quality towels are bulky and take a long time to dry. I cut a cheap, thin bath towel in half and sewed the edges. We each use one half as our towel. It is a little skimpy at the beach, but they pack into a small space and dry quickly.

I tried "camping" or "pack" towels and found them less absorbent than my half-towels and they also took longer to dry. Some cyclists like to bring linen dish towels or thin terry hand towels. I have even heard of minimalist cyclotourists who use their T-shirts as towels.

Insect Repellent

This can be a controversial subject. Anything that kills a bug is not likely to be very good for you either. On the other hand, it is down right nasty to be plagued by a swarm of biting gnats or mosquitoes. We carry DEET, a highly noxious chemical that dissolves spandex. However, we have had the same one-ounce bottle for 20 years so I guess we are not using that much. We rarely need it and use just a tiny drop and smear it around very thinly. Do not get any on any material made of elastic. It will begin to fall apart before your eyes.

Long clothing with pant legs tucked into your socks will also keep bugs away. We have mosquito netting to place over our heads and have been very grateful for it on more than one occasion.

Medications

Consider your normal drug consumption. I get headaches fairly often so I bring an analgesic, usually ibuprofen. I also have hay fever, so I bring anti-histamines and decongestants.

What about you? Do you get motion sickness? How about indigestion or constipation? It is always a good idea to carry something for diarrhea. Digestive problems are the most common illnesses suffered by travelers. And do not forget to take your vitamins!

Be sure you have enough of all of your prescription medications and bring the prescription itself in case you need more. I have never been asked to produce the Rx for drugs but I have heard that this sometimes happens when clearing customs.

I also carry an extra pair of prescription eyeglasses and the prescription. I am functionally blind without my specs and have a phobia about losing or breaking them. I have not yet, but you never know…

Personal Identification and Other Papers

You should always carry a driver's license or similar identification. Of course, you will need a passport if you are traveling out of your home country. It is a very good idea to take your health insurance card if you have one. Also, do not forget to take any discount cards you own, such as student ID, senior citizen cards, hostel cards, or anything else that will get you a deal somewhere.

Money

Money comes in many forms, some more convenient than others. Some forms of money even have a different value than others.

I do not recommend getting local currency before you leave home. You will find an exchange booth in every major airport operating at almost all hours of the day and night. Yes, you may find a line, but it is still less hassle than arranging to get currency at home and you will get a better rate.

Carrying a large sum of cash is nerve wracking at the least. You will need local currency for many of your purchases but do not carry more cash than you can afford to lose.

Traveler's checks remain a popular form of traveling money. They are relatively inexpensive and many places offer members free checks. And of course they can be replaced if they are lost or stolen. However, not all traveler's checks are created equal. American Express, Thomas Cook, and Visa are the most universally accepted.

Many hotels, restaurants, and stores accept major credit cards. You can also get cash advances on your cards although that is expensive. Just getting cash advances can be a time-consuming paperwork struggle if you are traveling to a foreign country. Usually using an ATM (Automatic Teller Machines) to get a cash advance is the simplest route. Most ATMs are programmed to accept MacPlus, Cirrus, Visa, Mastercard, and American Express cards. In contrast to traveler's checks, American Express credit cards are not as valuable as Visa and Mastercard.

We used to carry traveler's checks as our main source of funding on our trips. We usually do not bother to get them anymore because ATMs have become so ubiquitous. There is a fee for an ATM transaction outside of your home base. It can be as little as $1 or as high as $6. But it can be smaller than the combined fee of buying and cashing the traveler's checks and is certainly less than cash advances on a credit card. Each transaction is charged the same fee regardless of the amount. Many ATM cards can also be used as a credit card.

The number printed in the newspaper stating the exchange rate is not the rate you will receive. Even if the agency tells you that they are not charging you a fee, there is a fee built into the exchange rate itself. Banks usually give the best exchange rate, although that varies in some countries. The rate you receive on your ATM card will be among the best available. The rate charged by your credit card company will be good, but check to see if the merchant adds a fee for credit card purchases. It is possible that you will get a better deal if you pay with currency.

Personal Items

I always bring a small journal to record my trip. This brings memories flooding back when I read them years later. All kinds of details can be captured and replayed again and again. Do not forget to bring a pen.

If we think we will be spending much idle time, we will bring other toys and distractions. There are many travel games from crossword puzzles to chess that are available in small, light travel versions. Frequently I bring a paperback book relevant to my destination. I brought "Our Man in Havana" to Cuba, for example, which makes a reference to one of the hotels we stayed in.

Deciding What to Leave at Home

I have tried to tell you everything I can think of that might be useful on a bicycle tour. Now, I am going to tell you to leave as much of it at home as you can. Just because you can fit an item in your pack and it m*ight* be helpful does not mean you should bring it with you.

Ultimately, you are the best judge of what you will bring. Listen to your inner cyclist and do what he or she says.

Loading Your Packs and the Bicycle

OK, you have dragged everything out and it lies strewn around the living room floor. How do you get it all into the packs?

The bike will be the most stable and easy to handle with the weight as low as possible. Tools are heavy, but you may need them on the road. Will they fit into a lower outside pocket? perhaps you can leave the tools you are most likely to want close at hand and put the others on the bottom of the main compartment.

Food is also usually heavy. Things for dinner or the next day can go on the bottom. The same is true for most of your toilet kit. Keep items like sunscreen handy and put the rest away.

We use compression bags for our sleeping bags and put them into the main compartment, out of the way. Our backpacker tent with its short poles also fits in the main compartment along with stuff sacks with clothes. This will leave your rack top free for items you may need during the day. When you stop for lunch, it is a nuisance to have to take off the sleeping bags just to get at the salami.

Try to load around 60 percent of the weight in the rear panniers and 35–40 percent in the front. The handlebar bag should hold no more than 5 percent. The more weight you have in front, especially up high on the handlebars, the harder it will be to steer.

Straps are more stable than bungees. However, bungees push in on the gear it is holding. You can loosen bungees momentarily by pulling on them. I use bungees for my jacket or other items I will be pulling off and putting on during the day. I use straps for things I want to remain stable for the entire ride, such as any camping gear attached to the rack. Straps and bungees are also great for keeping your packs together when you use other transportation, such as trains, ferries, or airplanes.

10.

Michael and Pat's Lists

Everything we Took to Turkey and Utah, with Explanations

The answer to the question "What shall I take?" depends very much on where you are going. It also depends on what you are planning to do once you arrive. Let me compare the lists of the items we packed for two different tours: a three-week trip to Turkey and the Greek Islands and a two-week tour of southwestern Utah and the North Rim of the Grand Canyon.

The first was a tour that included 5 days in the very cosmopolitan city of Istanbul, a week of bike touring down the Turkish coast and a little over a week ferrying around the Greek Islands. This was a hard trip to pack for because of the diversity. In Istanbul, we wanted to look presentable in "nicer" restaurants and also to the conservative Moslems when we visited their mosques. Certainly, this meant we needed clothes other than the usual cycling shorts and jerseys. However, we needed those as well. This meant bringing along more clothing than usual. We brought camping equipment for the leg down the coast, but to save some weight and room in the packs, we brought no cooking gear. We also wanted beach wear for the Greek Islands. And since we were hopping from one ferry to another, we needed to have our bikes packed with as few pieces of luggage as possible.

Cycle touring is not a widespread activity in Turkey even among foreign tourists. When we met people in the countryside, they were greatly amused by our silly helmets, bright-colored clothes and fancy bikes loaded up with gear. Turkey is not as attuned to the needs of cyclists as some other countries are, and it was necessary for us to be very adaptable. Istanbul is a horrible place to bicycle and even the country roads could be daunting, because drivers are simply not used to bikes. We had to be patient and careful.

Utah was a tour of a different color. Nobody cared what we wore so modesty or offending someone's sensibilities was not an issue. We camped about half the time, sometimes in the middle of nowhere. We needed to be able to cook a hot meal in the high altitudes after the sun went down. We went in September and traveled from St. George, Utah, at elevation 2,900 ft to as high as 10,600 ft at Cedar Breaks National Monument and back down to St. George. Temperatures in St. George were around 90 degrees F (32 degrees C) and we began the tour in shorts and sleeveless shirts. A week later, when we woke at a campground below Cedar Breaks at 8,500 ft, there was frost on the ground and the temperature was 29 degrees F (–2 degrees C). We brought rain jackets, down vests, stocking caps and warm gloves. We had tights, long underwear, and wind pants. All on at the same time. As we pedaled and the sun came out, we dropped one layer at a time. By the time we got back to St. George, we were in sleeveless shirts and shorts again. Packing the right clothing was just as difficult as it had been in Turkey, but for completely different reasons.

Equipment we took to Turkey and the Greek Islands. (Items with * were also took to SW Utah)

Bikes and Equipment:

◻ Two Bikes*

◻ Two pair of rear panniers*

◻ Two handlebar bags*

◻ Four water bottles*

◻ Two racks*

◻ Two cyclometers* (although I bought a new one with altimeter for Utah)

◻ Two bells*

- 1 head lamp* (we took two to Utah
- 2 rear flashers*
- 2 cables and 2 combination locks*
- 2 small bungees to strap items to the rack*
- several long straps to strap the panniers together for transport on the plane*

Tools:

- Several yards of duct tape wound into a small wad*
- Frame pump*
- 2 extra inner tubes*
- Plastic tire levers*
- Patch kit with extra patches*
- Set of Allen keys
- 4-inch adjustable wrench*
- Channel-lock pliers*
- Chain tool
- 9 mm socket and handle for seatpost
- Multi-size combination bicycle wrench/spanner*
- Link for chain*
- Grease in an empty film canister*
- Crank extractor*
- Hyperglide cassette remover
- Presta to Schrader pump adapter*

Clothing, Pat:

- 2 pair of walking shorts (nylon)* (brought 1 pair to Utah)
- Bike shoes (for use with toeclips)

- 1 pair sports sandals*
- Four T-shirts (2 nylon, 2 cotton/poly-blend)
- 2 pair terry lined sport socks*
- 2 pair black cotton socks*
- 4 pair cotton panties*
- 2 bras*
- 1 helmet*
- 1 pair black nylon windpants*
- 1 cotton/poly blend turtleneck
- 1 crushable rayon jumper (can be worn alone, with T-shirt, or turtleneck)
- 1 pair fingerless bike gloves*
- 1 nylon windbreaker*
- 1 rain jacket*
- 1 swimsuit*
- 1 pair of inexpensive earrings and matching necklace
- 1 pair black pantyhose
- Straw hat with chin strap (crushed to a pulp by the end of the trip!)

Clothing, Michael:

- 1 pair Lycra bike shorts*
- 1 pair cotton walking shorts
- 2 cotton/poly blend T-shirts
- 1 cotton/poly blend polo shirt*
- 3 pair underwear*
- 1 pair black socks*
- 3 pair sport socks*
- 1 long-sleeve dress shirt

- ◻ 1 pair polyester dress pants
- ◻ 1 nylon jacket*
- ◻ 1 helmet*
- ◻ 1 pair long nylon pants with pockets*
- ◻ 1 cotton/ poly blend turtleneck*
- ◻ 1 wool knit tie (not used)
- ◻ 1 baseball cap
- ◻ 1 pair black athletic shoes
- ◻ 1 pair sports sandals*
- ◻ 1 swimsuit*
- ◻ 1 pair fingerless bike gloves*

Here is all of our gear packed for transport by plane.

Toiletries:

- ◻ Hair brush*

- ◻ Full bottle of general purpose shampoo* (brought smaller bottle to Utah)

- ◻ 1 shaver with ten disposable cartridges*

- ◻ 2 toothbrushes*

- ◻ dental floss*

- ◻ 1 tube toothpaste*

- ◻ lip gloss with 8 SPF

- ◻ lip gloss with 18 SPF*

- ◻ several Band-Aids*

- ◻ a pack of steristrips*

- ◻ sample size bottle of moisturizer*

- ◻ Medications:
    Ibuprofen*
    Motion sickness tablets*
    Antihistamine/decongestants (12 hour)*
    Antidiarrheal tablets*

- ◻ 2 half-towels*

- ◻ Make-up

- ◻ 1 eye shadow, mascara, eye liner pencil*

- ◻ Insect repellent*

- ◻ Q-tips*

- ◻ Tampons*

- ◻ RX for glasses for Pat and Michael*

- ◻ Clip-on sunglasses for Pat*

- ◻ Non-RX sunglasses for Michael*

- ◻ Toilet paper in plastic bag*

Miscellaneous:

- A 35-mm camera with 2 lenses (28–70 and 65–210) and minipod*
- Ten 24-exposure rolls of film*
- Turkish phrase book
- Pages slit out of guidebook to Turkey
- Pages slit out of guidebook to Istanbul
- Pages slit out of guidebook to Greek Islands
- Map of west Turkish coast
- City maps of Istanbul and Izmir, Turkey
- Personal journal *
- Pens *
- Fanny pack*
- Airplane comfort pack (inflatable head pillow, eyeshades, and ear plugs)
- 2 Swiss army knives: 1 with scissors for toiletry bag, 1 with Phillips screwdriver for tool kit*
- A few varied needles and 3 small spools of thread white, black, and sail thread*
- Small compass*
- 5 large trash bags*
- 6 large ziploc bags*
- 6 sandwich size ziploc bags*
- 6 stuff sacks*
- Extra batteries for lamps, camera*
- Passports
- Cash*
- Traveler's checks
- driver's license*
- Credit card*

◻ ATM card*

◻ Camping gear
　　1 camping set of spoon, knife, and fork* (brought two to Utah)
　　Butane lighter*
　　2 summer-weight sleeping bags
　　1 biking tent and poles (3.5 pounds)*

Panniers weighed about 25 pounds each pair, Handlebar bags weighed about 5 pounds each

Equipment we brought to SW Utah and Grand Canyon but not to Turkey:

Bikes and equipment:

◻ 2 cyclometers (1 with altimeter)

Tools:

◻ "Alien" Tool
　　2, 2.5, 3, 4, 5, 6 mm hex wrenches, 8 mm crank bolt hex wrench,
　　8, 9, 10 mm box wrenches, 10 mm heavy-duty box wrench,
　　universal chain tool, Phillips and flat head screwdrivers,
　　stainless steel knife, bottle opener, 2 spoke wrenches (14g and
　　15g), 2 tire levers in a tool that is 4 in. x 2 in. x 1 in., weighing
　　about a half a pound. This replaces many of the tools brought to
　　Turkey

◻ Spare Kevlar spoke

◻ 6 latex gloves

◻ Interchangeable head screwdriver

◻ Crank extractor

◻ 14 & 15 mm socket wrench for crank arm

◻ 1 set extra brake pads

Total weight: 3 lbs, size 10 in. x 5 in. x 2 in. pouch

Clothing, Pat

- 1 pair Lycra bike shorts
- 1 pair tights
- Rain pants
- Polarguard thermal pants
- 2 pair biking socks
- 1 pair "dress" socks
- 1 pair heavy wool socks
- Down vest
- Stocking hat
- Long-fingered biking gloves
- Bike shoes with cleats
- Canvas sneakers
- 2 short-sleeve biking jerseys
- 2 long-sleeve biking jerseys

Clothing, Michael:

- 1 pair tights
- Rain pants
- Rain jacket
- Down vest
- Stocking hat
- Long-fingered biking gloves
- Bike shoes with cleats
- Canvas sneakers
- 1 short-sleeve biking jersey
- 1 sleeveless biking jersey

□ 1 long-sleeve biking jersey

Toiletry bag:

□ Electric rechargeable shaver

□ Lip balm (with no SPF)

□ Lip balm with 25 SPF

□ Vitamins

Miscellaneous:

□ Topo maps of our tour area

□ Pages slit out of guide books

□ Camping Gear:
    Ground Tarp
    Winter-weight down bags
    Coleman Peak 1 single burner white gas backpacking stove
    2 aluminum pots and lids
    2 plastic bowls
    2 cups
    1 large spoon
    Burgundy Beef freeze dried dinner for two (Did not use)
    2 freeze-dried omelets (used 1)

A List of One's Own: Checklist for Touring

This is an edited version of my "Master List." It is intended to be a guide so that you won't forget anything. I have never brought every one of these items along on any trip and I don't expect you to either. Frequently, I have packed fewer than half of them. In fact, there are items on this list that I do not even own. They are included because you may be interested in them. Use the information in this book and your own judgment to whittle the list into one that includes enough to keep you happy but not too much to carry. I have included some blank lines at the end to write in items of your own choosing. I have also included a series of boxes for you to check off for each trip.

Don't forget the Bike!

Packs:

[ ][ ][ ][ ][ ][ ][ ] Rear panniers

[ ][ ][ ][ ][ ][ ][ ] Front pannier

[ ][ ][ ][ ][ ][ ][ ] Handlebar bag

[ ][ ][ ][ ][ ][ ][ ] seatpost bag

[ ][ ][ ][ ][ ][ ][ ] Frame pack

[ ][ ][ ][ ][ ][ ][ ] Rack-top pack

[ ][ ][ ][ ][ ][ ][ ] Oh, and the rack(s)

[ ][ ][ ][ ][ ][ ][ ] _____

We really felt the weight of our packs climbing hills in San Francisco.

[ ][ ][ ][ ][ ][ ][ ][ ] _____

[ ][ ][ ][ ][ ][ ][ ][ ] _____

Attachments:

[ ][ ][ ][ ][ ][ ][ ][ ] Water bottles and cages

[ ][ ][ ][ ][ ][ ][ ][ ] Cyclometers

[ ][ ][ ][ ][ ][ ][ ][ ] Bell

[ ][ ][ ][ ][ ][ ][ ][ ] Headlight

[ ][ ][ ][ ][ ][ ][ ][ ] Rear light or flasher

[ ][ ][ ][ ][ ][ ][ ][ ] Cables and/or bike lock and/or padlock

[ ][ ][ ][ ][ ][ ][ ][ ] Bungees

[ ][ ][ ][ ][ ][ ][ ][ ] Straps

[ ][ ][ ][ ][ ][ ][ ][ ] _____

[ ][ ][ ][ ][ ][ ][ ][ ] _____

[ ][ ][ ][ ][ ][ ][ ][ ] _____

[ ][ ][ ][ ][ ][ ][ ][ ] _____

Tools:

Option A:

[ ][ ][ ][ ][ ][ ][ ][ ] Plastic tire levers

[ ][ ][ ][ ][ ][ ][ ][ ] Allen keys (Hex wrenches) to fit your bike

[ ][ ][ ][ ][ ][ ][ ][ ] Flat head screwdriver

[ ][ ][ ][ ][ ][ ][ ][ ] Philip's head screwdriver

[ ][ ][ ][ ][ ][ ][ ][ ] Chain tool

[ ][ ][ ][ ][ ][ ][ ][ ] 9 mm socket and handle

[ ][ ][ ][ ][ ][ ][ ][ ] Spoke wrench

Option B:

[ ][ ][ ][ ][ ][ ][ ][ ] "Alien Tool" TM (Topeak) (2, 2.5, 3, 4, 5, 6 hex wrenches, 8 mm crank bolt hex wrench, 8, 9, 10 mm box wrenches,

10 mm heavy-duty box wrench, universal chain tool, Phillips and flat head screwdrivers, stainless steel knife, bottle opener, 2 spoke wrenches (14 g and 15 g), 2 tire levers in a tool that measures 4 in. x 2 in. x 1 in. and weighs about a half a pound)

Use Option A or Option B above Plus the following:

[ ][ ][ ][ ][ ][ ][ ][ ] Spare conventional or Kevlar spoke

[ ][ ][ ][ ][ ][ ][ ][ ] Patch kit with extra patches(make sure the glue has not evaporated)

[ ][ ][ ][ ][ ][ ][ ][ ] Pump

[ ][ ][ ][ ][ ][ ][ ][ ] 2 extra inner tubes and foldable spare tire

[ ][ ][ ][ ][ ][ ][ ][ ] Several yards of duct tape wound into a small wad

[ ][ ][ ][ ][ ][ ][ ][ ] New master link for chain

[ ][ ][ ][ ][ ][ ][ ][ ] Lubricant (grease, oil, wax)

[ ][ ][ ][ ][ ][ ][ ][ ] Freewheel/Cassette tool

[ ][ ][ ][ ][ ][ ][ ][ ] Presta /Schrader pump adapter

[ ][ ][ ][ ][ ][ ][ ][ ] Latex gloves

[ ][ ][ ][ ][ ][ ][ ][ ] Crank arm extractor

[ ][ ][ ][ ][ ][ ][ ][ ] 14 or 15 mm socket wrench (correct size for your crank)

[ ][ ][ ][ ][ ][ ][ ][ ] Extra brake pads

[ ][ ][ ][ ][ ][ ][ ][ ] Four inch adjustable wrench

[ ][ ][ ][ ][ ][ ][ ][ ] Medium size channel lock wrench

[ ][ ][ ][ ][ ][ ][ ][ ] Cone wrench

[ ][ ][ ][ ][ ][ ][ ][ ] Small roll of bailing wire

[ ][ ][ ][ ][ ][ ][ ][ ] Spare brake/derailleur cable

Total weight: 3 lbs, size 10 in. x 5 in. x 2 in. pouch

[ ][ ][ ][ ][ ][ ][ ][ ] _____

[ ][ ][ ][ ][ ][ ][ ][ ] _____

[ ][ ][ ][ ][ ][ ][ ][ ] _____

[ ][ ][ ][ ][ ][ ][ ][ ] ——————————

[ ][ ][ ][ ][ ][ ][ ][ ] ——————————

Bicycle Clothing

[ ][ ][ ][ ][ ][ ][ ][ ] Cycling shorts or suitable walking shorts and bike liners

[ ][ ][ ][ ][ ][ ][ ][ ] Cycling tights

[ ][ ][ ][ ][ ][ ][ ][ ] Bike shoes

[ ][ ][ ][ ][ ][ ][ ][ ] Short-sleeve Jersey or T-shirt

[ ][ ][ ][ ][ ][ ][ ][ ] long-sleeve jersey or T-shirt

[ ][ ][ ][ ][ ][ ][ ][ ] Sport socks

[ ][ ][ ][ ][ ][ ][ ][ ] Helmet

[ ][ ][ ][ ][ ][ ][ ][ ] Wind pants

[ ][ ][ ][ ][ ][ ][ ][ ] Wind breaker jacket

[ ][ ][ ][ ][ ][ ][ ][ ] Rain pants

[ ][ ][ ][ ][ ][ ][ ][ ] Rain jacket

[ ][ ][ ][ ][ ][ ][ ][ ] Rain over-booties

[ ][ ][ ][ ][ ][ ][ ][ ] Fingerless cycling gloves

[ ][ ][ ][ ][ ][ ][ ][ ] Long-fingered cycling gloves

[ ][ ][ ][ ][ ][ ][ ][ ] Sports bra

[ ][ ][ ][ ][ ][ ][ ][ ] Sunglasses

[ ][ ][ ][ ][ ][ ][ ][ ] Visor or hat with brim

[ ][ ][ ][ ][ ][ ][ ][ ] Handkerchief

[ ][ ][ ][ ][ ][ ][ ][ ] Head scarf

[ ][ ][ ][ ][ ][ ][ ][ ] ——————————

[ ][ ][ ][ ][ ][ ][ ][ ] ——————————

[ ][ ][ ][ ][ ][ ][ ][ ] ——————————

[ ][ ][ ][ ][ ][ ][ ][ ] ——————————

[ ][ ][ ][ ][ ][ ][ ][ ] ——————————

[ ][ ][ ][ ][ ][ ][ ][ ] _____

[ ][ ][ ][ ][ ][ ][ ][ ] _____

[ ][ ][ ][ ][ ][ ][ ][ ] _____

[ ][ ][ ][ ][ ][ ][ ][ ] _____

[ ][ ][ ][ ][ ][ ][ ][ ] _____

Clothing, Off the Bike

[ ][ ][ ][ ][ ][ ][ ][ ] Long Pants

[ ][ ][ ][ ][ ][ ][ ][ ] Shorts

[ ][ ][ ][ ][ ][ ][ ][ ] Crushable skirt or dress

[ ][ ][ ][ ][ ][ ][ ][ ] T-shirts/Polo-type shirts

[ ][ ][ ][ ][ ][ ][ ][ ] long-sleeve shirts/dress shirt

[ ][ ][ ][ ][ ][ ][ ][ ] Sweater

[ ][ ][ ][ ][ ][ ][ ][ ] Jacket

[ ][ ][ ][ ][ ][ ][ ][ ] Sandals

[ ][ ][ ][ ][ ][ ][ ][ ] Walking shoes

[ ][ ][ ][ ][ ][ ][ ][ ] Socks

[ ][ ][ ][ ][ ][ ][ ][ ] Underpants

[ ][ ][ ][ ][ ][ ][ ][ ] Bras

[ ][ ][ ][ ][ ][ ][ ][ ] Swimsuit

[ ][ ][ ][ ][ ][ ][ ][ ] Pantyhose

[ ][ ][ ][ ][ ][ ][ ][ ] Hat

[ ][ ][ ][ ][ ][ ][ ][ ] Thermal underwear

[ ][ ][ ][ ][ ][ ][ ][ ] Down vest

[ ][ ][ ][ ][ ][ ][ ][ ] Warm gloves or mittens

[ ][ ][ ][ ][ ][ ][ ][ ] Warm hat

[ ][ ][ ][ ][ ][ ][ ][ ] Belt

[ ][ ][ ][ ][ ][ ][ ][ ] _____

[ ][ ][ ][ ][ ][ ][ ][ ] _____

[ ][ ][ ][ ][ ][ ][ ][ ] _____

[ ][ ][ ][ ][ ][ ][ ][ ] _____

[ ][ ][ ][ ][ ][ ][ ][ ] _____

[ ][ ][ ][ ][ ][ ][ ][ ] _____

[ ][ ][ ][ ][ ][ ][ ][ ] _____

[ ][ ][ ][ ][ ][ ][ ][ ] _____

Toiletries:

[ ][ ][ ][ ][ ][ ][ ][ ] Hair brush/comb

[ ][ ][ ][ ][ ][ ][ ][ ] Shampoo (to be used as general purpose soap)

[ ][ ][ ][ ][ ][ ][ ][ ] Shaver

[ ][ ][ ][ ][ ][ ][ ][ ] Toothbrush

[ ][ ][ ][ ][ ][ ][ ][ ] Dental floss

[ ][ ][ ][ ][ ][ ][ ][ ] Toothpaste

[ ][ ][ ][ ][ ][ ][ ][ ] Lip gloss (preferably with SPF)

[ ][ ][ ][ ][ ][ ][ ][ ] Several Band-Aids

[ ][ ][ ][ ][ ][ ][ ][ ] Pack of steristrips

[ ][ ][ ][ ][ ][ ][ ][ ] Hand lotion/petroleum jelly

[ ][ ][ ][ ][ ][ ][ ][ ] Towels

[ ][ ][ ][ ][ ][ ][ ][ ] Make-up

[ ][ ][ ][ ][ ][ ][ ][ ] Insect repellent

[ ][ ][ ][ ][ ][ ][ ][ ] Cotton swabs

[ ][ ][ ][ ][ ][ ][ ][ ] Tampons

[ ][ ][ ][ ][ ][ ][ ][ ] Prescription for glasses

[ ][ ][ ][ ][ ][ ][ ][ ] Extra pair of glasses

[ ][ ][ ][ ][ ][ ][ ][ ] Toilet paper

[ ][ ][ ][ ][ ][ ][ ][ ] Eye wash solution

[ ][ ][ ][ ][ ][ ][ ][ ] _____

[ ][ ][ ][ ][ ][ ][ ][ ] _____

[ ][ ][ ][ ][ ][ ][ ][ ] _____

[ ][ ][ ][ ][ ][ ][ ][ ] _____

[ ][ ][ ][ ][ ][ ][ ][ ] _____

Medications:

[ ][ ][ ][ ][ ][ ][ ][ ] Ibuprofen/aspirin/acetaminophen

[ ][ ][ ][ ][ ][ ][ ][ ] Motion sickness tablets

[ ][ ][ ][ ][ ][ ][ ][ ] Antihistamine/decongestants

[ ][ ][ ][ ][ ][ ][ ][ ] Antidiarrheal tablets

[ ][ ][ ][ ][ ][ ][ ][ ] Laxatives

[ ][ ][ ][ ][ ][ ][ ][ ] Prescription medications and prescriptions

[ ][ ][ ][ ][ ][ ][ ][ ] Vitamins

[ ][ ][ ][ ][ ][ ][ ][ ] _____

[ ][ ][ ][ ][ ][ ][ ][ ] _____

[ ][ ][ ][ ][ ][ ][ ][ ] _____

[ ][ ][ ][ ][ ][ ][ ][ ] _____

[ ][ ][ ][ ][ ][ ][ ][ ] _____

Miscellaneous:

[ ][ ][ ][ ][ ][ ][ ][ ] Maps: Road, Cycling, Topos, City plans, etc.

[ ][ ][ ][ ][ ][ ][ ][ ] Camera/lenses/tripod/bag/film

[ ][ ][ ][ ][ ][ ][ ][ ] Phrase book(s)

[ ][ ][ ][ ][ ][ ][ ][ ] Pages slit out of guidebook

[ ][ ][ ][ ][ ][ ][ ][ ] Maps

[ ][ ][ ][ ][ ][ ][ ][ ] Personal journal and pens/pencils

[ ][ ][ ][ ][ ][ ][ ][ ] Fanny pack

[ ][ ][ ][ ][ ][ ][ ][ ] Day pack

[ ][ ][ ][ ][ ][ ][ ][ ] Airplane "comfort pack" (inflatable head pillow, eyeshades and ear plugs)

[ ][ ][ ][ ][ ][ ][ ][ ] Multi-blade utility knives

[ ][ ][ ][ ][ ][ ][ ][ ] A few varied needles, small spools of thread

[ ][ ][ ][ ][ ][ ][ ][ ] Compass

[ ][ ][ ][ ][ ][ ][ ][ ] Several large trash bags

[ ][ ][ ][ ][ ][ ][ ][ ] Several large food storage bags

[ ][ ][ ][ ][ ][ ][ ][ ] Sandwich size ziploc bags

[ ][ ][ ][ ][ ][ ][ ][ ] Extra Stuff sacks

[ ][ ][ ][ ][ ][ ][ ][ ] Passports

[ ][ ][ ][ ][ ][ ][ ][ ] Cash

[ ][ ][ ][ ][ ][ ][ ][ ] Traveler's checks

[ ][ ][ ][ ][ ][ ][ ][ ] Driver's license

[ ][ ][ ][ ][ ][ ][ ][ ] Credit card

[ ][ ][ ][ ][ ][ ][ ][ ] ATM card

[ ][ ][ ][ ][ ][ ][ ][ ] Travel games and/or playing cards

[ ][ ][ ][ ][ ][ ][ ][ ] Paperback book

[ ][ ][ ][ ][ ][ ][ ][ ] Mosquito netting

[ ][ ][ ][ ][ ][ ][ ][ ] Extra batteries for lights, camera, etc.

[ ][ ][ ][ ][ ][ ][ ][ ] _____

[ ][ ][ ][ ][ ][ ][ ][ ] _____

[ ][ ][ ][ ][ ][ ][ ][ ] _____

[ ][ ][ ][ ][ ][ ][ ][ ] _____

[ ][ ][ ][ ][ ][ ][ ][ ] _____

[ ][ ][ ][ ][ ][ ][ ][ ] _____

[ ][ ][ ][ ][ ][ ][ ][ ] _____

[ ][ ][ ][ ][ ][ ][ ][ ] _____

[ ][ ][ ][ ][ ][ ][ ][ ] _____

Camping gear

[ ][ ][ ][ ][ ][ ][ ][ ] Camping set of spoon, knife, and fork

[ ][ ][ ][ ][ ][ ][ ][ ] Backpackers stove and fuel

[ ][ ][ ][ ][ ][ ][ ][ ] Butane lighter and/or waterproof matches

[ ][ ][ ][ ][ ][ ][ ][ ] Sleeping bags (Winter, 3-season or Summer?)

[ ][ ][ ][ ][ ][ ][ ][ ] Tent, poles, stakes, and rain fly

[ ][ ][ ][ ][ ][ ][ ][ ] Ground tarp

[ ][ ][ ][ ][ ][ ][ ][ ] Pads for under sleeping bags

[ ][ ][ ][ ][ ][ ][ ][ ] Waterproof bags for sleeping bags

[ ][ ][ ][ ][ ][ ][ ][ ] Camping-weight pots and lids

[ ][ ][ ][ ][ ][ ][ ][ ] Plastic bowls or camping dishes

[ ][ ][ ][ ][ ][ ][ ][ ] Cups

[ ][ ][ ][ ][ ][ ][ ][ ] Large serving spoon

[ ][ ][ ][ ][ ][ ][ ][ ] Dish scrubbing pads

[ ][ ][ ][ ][ ][ ][ ][ ] Candle lantern

[ ][ ][ ][ ][ ][ ][ ][ ] Multiblade utility knife

[ ][ ][ ][ ][ ][ ][ ][ ] Water treatment gear (e.g. iodine tablets, filters, etc.)

[ ][ ][ ][ ][ ][ ][ ][ ] Short length of lightweight rope

[ ][ ][ ][ ][ ][ ][ ][ ] Pot holders

[ ][ ][ ][ ][ ][ ][ ][ ] Flashlight/head lamp

[ ][ ][ ][ ][ ][ ][ ][ ] _____

[ ][ ][ ][ ][ ][ ][ ][ ] _____

[ ][ ][ ][ ][ ][ ][ ][ ] _____

[ ][ ][ ][ ][ ][ ][ ][ ] _____

[ ][ ][ ][ ][ ][ ][ ][ ] _____

[ ][ ][ ][ ][ ][ ][ ][ ] _____

[ ][ ][ ][ ][ ][ ][ ][ ] _____

[ ][ ][ ][ ][ ][ ][ ][ ] _____

[ ][ ][ ][ ][ ][ ][ ][ ] _____

Food

Always carry enough for at least one meal plus snacks

[ ][ ][ ][ ][ ][ ][ ][ ] Nuts

[ ][ ][ ][ ][ ][ ][ ][ ] Dried fruit

[ ][ ][ ][ ][ ][ ][ ][ ] Bite-sized candy that won't squish or melt

[ ][ ][ ][ ][ ][ ][ ][ ] Hard rolls or bagels

[ ][ ][ ][ ][ ][ ][ ][ ] Food bars, e.g. sports, granola, candy, breakfast

[ ][ ][ ][ ][ ][ ][ ][ ] Preserved, hard meats (e.g. salami)

[ ][ ][ ][ ][ ][ ][ ][ ] Block cheese

[ ][ ][ ][ ][ ][ ][ ][ ] Peanut butter and jelly

[ ][ ][ ][ ][ ][ ][ ][ ] Hard fresh fruit, i.e. apples, oranges

[ ][ ][ ][ ][ ][ ][ ][ ] Cookies

[ ][ ][ ][ ][ ][ ][ ][ ] Tea bags/ hot chocolate/coffee

[ ][ ][ ][ ][ ][ ][ ][ ] Sugar/creamer

[ ][ ][ ][ ][ ][ ][ ][ ] Freeze-dried foods

[ ][ ][ ][ ][ ][ ][ ][ ] Packaged soups

[ ][ ][ ][ ][ ][ ][ ][ ] Sports Drinks

[ ][ ][ ][ ][ ][ ][ ][ ] _____

[ ][ ][ ][ ][ ][ ][ ][ ] _____

[ ][ ][ ][ ][ ][ ][ ][ ] _____

[ ][ ][ ][ ][ ][ ][ ][ ] _____

[ ][ ][ ][ ][ ][ ][ ][ ] _____

[ ][ ][ ][ ][ ][ ][ ][ ] _____

[ ][ ][ ][ ][ ][ ][ ][ ] _____

[ ][ ][ ][ ][ ][ ][ ][ ] _____

[ ][ ][ ][ ][ ][ ][ ][ ] _____

[ ][ ][ ][ ][ ][ ][ ][ ] _____

Part III

During the Tour

11.

Cycling Skills and Rules of the Road

I STARTED riding a bicycle when I was about six. Except for my "cool" period in my late teens and early twenties, I have been riding ever since. I took my first tour in 1982. Although I took a few tours in between, I did not start cycling seriously until 1990 when I started commuting to work by bicycle. In addition to the fifteen mile-a-day commute, Michael and I take a longer ride on most weekends, frequently with the Bicycling Club of Philadelphia. We also take at least one cycling vacation a year.

Commuting, more than touring, made me a seasoned cyclist. The daily minuet with traffic — motorists, pedestrians, in-line skaters, and other cyclists — has taught me about human relations as well as honing my cycling skills. Even after thousands of miles, my education still continues.

While there is no substitute for experience, you can learn quite a bit by listening to veteran bikers, many of whom are willing to share their knowledge. In the reference section I included some groups that provide worthwhile seminars, workshops, and classes. Also, consider joining a local bicycle club. The companionship increases the enjoyment and you can learn much from your fellow riders.

Rules of the Road

Lesson 1. Don't Go There!

Ultimately, the best advice on handling traffic is to avoid it by traveling on roads that have as little as possible. If the roads are different than you expected, check the map and see if you can come up with an alternative.

However, this is not always possible and there are some practices that will keep you safe and happy when it is necessary to mingle with those nasty brutes with internal combustion engines.

Act Like a Motorist, But Don't Forget You Are a Bicyclist

In most places, bicycles are granted the same rights and carry the same responsibilities as motorized traffic. Cyclists are expected to yield the right of way as a motorist would, ride in the same direction as cars, obey traffic signs and yield to pedestrians.

However, a bicycle is not a car. We cannot ride at the speed of automobile traffic and therefore we are expected to stay to the right side of the roadway. "As far to the right as is safe and practical," is the usual phrasing. There are also many motorists who do not recognize the rights of bicycles in the roadways. This means that bicyclists need to assess each situation and decide which action is best.

Be Predictable by Obeying Traffic Laws

No one wants to be involved in a collision, and one of the best ways to avoid one is to correctly predict the other person's next move. Traffic laws provide universal guidelines to help us do this. Most drivers at least know the rules of the road for cars, and if they see you acting like a car, it will be easier for them to anticipate your next move.

It Is Better to Be Safe than Legal

No one ever really owns the right of way. Rather, it is required that one party yield to the other. Give up the right of way if it will prevent a collision. This is as true of motorists and pedestrians as it is of bicyclists. However, a bicyclist will to come out of a car/bicycle collision with the most damage, so it is in your best interests to keep alert and be ready to react to someone else's unsafe or illegal maneuver.

Some motorists are concentrating on other cars and regard everyone else as irrelevant. These are the people who will refer to the bicycle they just hit as "coming out of nowhere." Making eye contact with a driver makes it less likely that you will be ignored, but the driver may still use poor judgment when predicting your speed or direction.

Do Not Hug the Curb

It is more likely that there will be debris, such as broken glass, tree branches, and other litter on the far right side of the road. That is also where storm sewers are located. If you are up against the curb, you have nowhere to go if the road is not clear directly ahead of you. Give yourself room to maneuver. You are also more visible to drivers.

Taking the Lane

There are times when you do not want to remain on the right side of the road. On very narrow roads where there is not enough room for a car to safely pass you, it is better not to tempt them by snuggling up to the curb. Ride in the middle of the lane until it is safe for them to pass.

The sign says it all.

Be Wary of Parked Cars

When you ride next to a line of parked cars, give yourself enough space to avoid an open car door. It is technically illegal to open a car door and step out into a traffic lane because it has the potential to cause a serious accident. But most of us do this routinely and too many people do not look first. Cyclists have been killed by opening car doors, and even minor mishaps can hurt you and damage the bicycle. While it helps to look for movement, car exhaust or lights, it is not always possible to see if there is someone in a car. Try to keep a distance of three feet from parked cars. If the road is too narrow to allow this, ride slowly and be prepared to stop quickly.

Do Not Weave In and Out Between Parked Cars

If there are breaks in a line of parked cars, do not weave into the open spaces. Continue riding in a straight line. If you pull over into the empty space, cars may assume you are not returning to traffic, they may lose sight of you, or they may misjudge how and when you will move back into the lane.

Be Alert at Intersections

Intersections are the most dangerous places for everyone — motorists, cyclists, and pedestrians. Sometimes it is hard to figure out who has the right of way. Sometimes you are dealing with a jerk who will challenge everyone. The first rule, as always, is be safe.

While drivers and bikers are supposed to use turn signals, many do not. Make eye contact with the driver and watch the car's wheels. Be wary when the wheels do not come to a complete stop or if there is any sign of changing direction.

Do not assume that a driver will not turn into you. Sometimes an idiot will pass a bicycle and swerve in front to turn right. Unfortunately, it is difficult to make predictions about a car you cannot see. Being aware of this possibility will help.

Signal Your Turns

Put your left arm straight out to the left to turn left. Put your right arm straight out to the right to turn right. Few people pay attention to the sign to indicate you are stopping, left arm out with forearm pointed down, but use it anyway. If you need to stop, be prepared to move out of traffic and off to the side as quickly as possible.

Make Left Turns Cautiously

With left turns, each situation is different. It is legally correct for a cyclist to turn left from a left-turn lane, and generally this is the best option. After completing the turn, ride directly into the right lane to get out of traffic as quickly as possible.

However, it is not always safe or easy to do this. Bicyclists always have the ability to pretend they are pedestrians by dismounting the bike and walking in the crosswalks. You get the same result by riding straight through the intersection and waiting at the opposite corner until it is safe to cross to the left.

Right-Turn Lanes Are for Turning Right

If you are continuing straight ahead, do not ride on the right side of a right-turn lane. Motorists may assume you are turning right and turn into your path. Sometimes motorists are not looking to their right when they turn. They are looking left at oncoming traffic and may not see you.

If you are going straight, either move to the far left hand side of the turning lane or to the right side of the straight-ahead lane, whichever has the least traffic.

Passing on the Right

Be very cautious when approaching an intersection with cars lined up waiting for their turn. If there is a bicycle lane or a large shoulder you can carefully creep upon the right. But watch the cars in front of you and stop if you see any movement. If you do not have enough room to pass safely, get behind the last car, right in the middle of the bumper. This will prevent any cars behind you from passing you too closely or turning right and hitting you.

Passing Buses and Trucks

You can safely pass trucks or buses on the right if there is a bike lane. However, even then be very cautious. These vehicles are wider and longer than cars and they have large blind spots close to the side of the vehicle. They also make wide right turns, sometimes from the left lane.

Buses also have blind spots on the left. If you want to pass a bus that has stopped to let passengers on or off move into the middle of the left lane. If the bus starts to move before you have passed completely, drop back and let the bus get ahead of you.

Riding in Groups

When riding with others, it is the responsibility of the person in back to avoid hitting the person in front, just as it is with cars. Keep enough distance between you and the next person so that if that person changes speed or direction, you will be able to avoid a collision. The person in front cannot see you. He or she does not know how close you are or how fast you are going. Pass on the left only and give warning. But remember that saying "Passing on the left" does not mean the right of way shifts to you. It is still your responsibility to pass safely.

Having said that, if there are cyclists behind you, signal if you are changing speed, turning, stopping or making any other change of movement. You can use hand signals or call out, "stopping" or "turning right."

Make Your Own Decisions

Approach each situation ready to decide for yourself what is best. It is always dangerous to let someone else do your thinking for you. Just because the person in front of you made it through the traffic light does not mean you should go also.

Stay Together

If one of your party falls behind, slow down or stop and wait. Your trip will be more fun if you stay together. It will make the slowest people in the party feel included and you will enjoy your experiences more if you share them with friends along the way.

Remember the Golden Rule: How Would You Want to Be Treated?

In any situation in which you are uncertain of the proper action, put yourself in the other person's position. How would you feel if you were a motorist or a pedestrian and someone did to you what you just did to them?

When you pass a pedestrian or another cyclist, give them warning far enough in advance so that they can react. A bicycle can move very quietly and it is easy to startle someone by whizzing past without warning.

It is really aggravating to be passed by a car that is too close. It is just as aggravating to be passed by a bike that is too close. You may know you are not going to hit them, but they might not be so sure.

Cycling Skills

A couple of months after a friend of mine joined a bicycle club, I asked how it was going. She said she was learning a lot from the club members. She could now ride standing up and was becoming comfortable looking behind her as she rode. She had even been complimented recently by another rider who told her she was getting much better a keeping a straight line as she rode. I was surprised at first because I did not think of those as skills to be learned; they just came automatically when you learned to ride a bicycle. My friend learned to ride a few years earlier, whereas I have been riding a bicycle for almost 40 years. Of course skills learned so long ago seem natural.

Those of you who have also been riding for a long time on the roads around town may want to skip the next couple of paragraphs, but for those of you who are new to the fine art of bicycling, here is my advice on developing competence and confidence in your bicycling abilities.

Looking Behind You

Being able to look behind you is an essential skill for riding in traffic. Always look behind when you pass, change to or from a turning lane or merge with other traffic. There is a trick to looking back. Keep your shoulders level. To sneak a quick peek to check traffic, sit up a bit, keep your hands on the handlebar and turn only your head to the left. If you need a better, longer look, keep your body as upright as possible and drop one hand from the handlebars to your side. Rotate your torso without leaning to the side. Lead with your shoulders, keeping them level.

Keeping a Straight Line

Riding in a straight line without wavering requires that you keep your body "quiet" while you ride. The less movement you make from your hips up, the straighter your line of direction. If you cannot pedal without rocking the bicycle, your seat is too high or the bike is too big.

Riding Out of the Saddle

Cycling in a standing position uses slightly different muscles than sitting. On a long trip, this can help relieve tired muscles. It also allows you to use all of your weight to push the pedals, giving you more power. This is helpful when you are climbing hills. Standing requires more energy though, and you will tire more quickly.

The trick to riding in a standing position is … well … there is no trick. Get a good, comfortable grip on the handlebars, straighten your legs, and keep pedaling.

You will see racers rock the bike back and forth when they stand. It should be obvious that you will not want to do that with a loaded touring bike.

Braking

A bicycle can go into a skid if you apply too much brake pressure all at once. Also, while it may be possible to put enough pressure on the wheel rims to stop them very quickly, the cyclist's momentum may carry him or her over the handlebars. Apply front and rear brakes with even pressure.

Play Games as You Ride

Take the time once in a while to play. Pick a nice, quiet street when you are not in a hurry and practice moves that you do not usually need.

It takes practice to develop skills that will help you maneuver quickly and safely. And knowing the limits of your ability as well as the bicycle's will give you confidence and make riding more fun. Practice sudden stops. Pretend to avoid hazards by weaving quickly. Roll down the street doing S-curves back and forth. Try taking sharp corners while pedaling and while coasting. All of these involve shifting your body weight to make the move as smooth as possible. Learn to use your whole body to move the bike.

Relax

Sometimes the best way to control the bike is to relax. If you are tense, you will tend to oversteer. Then you will need to steer back in the opposite direction and you will find yourself weaving. With full packs the effect is magnified.

Anticipate

Keep your eyes focused down the road a bit instead of directly in front of you. This will help you anticipate and prepare for situations before you are actually in them. Slow down before you get to an area where you will need more control. You have more maneuvering control when pedaling than coasting and you have the least control when you are braking.

Railroad and Trolley Tracks

When you encounter railroad and trolley tracks and cattle grates, cross as close to perpendicular to the tracks as possible. If you cross at a very shallow angle your wheel is more likely to get stuck in the track which might cause a fall. Grates and tracks are also very slippery when they are wet. Again, slow down ahead of time, pedal normally, and do not apply the brakes as you cross.

Pay Attention

In heavy traffic it is best to avoid checking the map, adjusting packs or drinking from your water bottle while riding. You will be less alert and less in control of your bike. Pull over to the side or onto the sidewalk, make whatever adjustment is necessary and then continue along the road.

Shifting Gears

Anticipate hills and shift ahead of time. It can be a chore to shift to a lower gear a couple pedal strokes after you have begun a hard climb. Sometimes the force can prevent your derailleur from changing gears or for the chain to pop off the rings.

You do not need to be a pro to be a good cyclist. All it really takes is common sense and a little experience.

12.

Transporting You and Your Bicycle

I FIND the process of getting from my home to the starting point of my tour to be a transforming experience. The time required to pack my gear and my bicycle, the struggle to get everything to the airport at a reasonable time, all the time-consuming, mind-absorbing activities required tend to cause a shift in my thinking. A long flight, especially a sleepless one, disrupts my body's schedule. A drastic change of climate or customs throws me off even more. When I emerge at the other end of my travel portal, I find that everything has changed. My job is gone. My house and daily routine are forgotten and I am ready to experience a new world. While it is more uncomfortable, I find that the more disruptive and the longer my transition has been, the more quickly I am prepared to accept my new "life."

Nonetheless, it is best to try to make the process as painless as possible. Getting you and your bicycle to the start of your tour can be very easy or a potential nightmare.

Getting There by Car

If you will drive a car to your destination, you have several possibilities. Some cars are large enough to carry bicycles without a rack. We used to have an old Chevy Suburban that could easily hold four bicycles standing upright in the back and still have room for four people and their gear. Now that we drive a Taurus station wagon, we have to remove the front wheels of the bike and we only have room for two.

Whether or not you can carry bicycles inside the car, you can consider a rack. There are racks that will fit on the trunk, hatchback or roof. If you want to carry more than two bikes, you will probably need a roof rack. The disadvantages of roof racks are that it can be difficult to get the bike up there and that you must be careful about places with low headroom. A friend of mine worked long and hard to build his dream bike and then destroyed it in a parking garage.

With trunk and hatchback racks, be careful to avoid scratching or otherwise damaging the bikes and the car. Padding, such as an old blanket, will help. Also, remember the bikes are there when you put the car in reverse.

Trains

Transporting bicycles by train can either be perfect or an exercise in frustration. In the U.S., there is slow movement toward acceptance of bicycles on trains. It depends on the company and the particular line. Trains with separate baggage cars will usually accept bicycles. Bicycles packed in cases may be easier to get on board. Generally, in the U.S., the farther west you go, the less trouble you have. Very few commuter trains allow bicycles during peak travel hours.

One book about cycling in Italy stated that the trains were a great way to travel with bicycles. We found that some of the trains will take them but they are not allowed on most. On one trip, our irate conductor was going to charge us. $100 for each bicycle. Fortunately, the other passengers in our compartment loudly berated him and chased him away. He said he would come back later, but he never did. It turns out that local trains will carry freight of any kind, including bicycles, but express trains are for hand-carried baggage only. Check ahead of time by contacting the railroad company or local bicycle clubs and cycling advocacy groups.

Buses

While you may have bad luck with metropolitan lines, it is usually easy to take your bike on an inter-city bus. Buses designed for long-distance travel frequently have a large compartment underneath where you can stow all of your gear. You will need to remove the panniers and push the bicycle in on its side.

A few long-distance buses have racks on the front that will hold a couple of bicycles. You will need to carry your packs onto the bus with you.

Ferries

Ferries are among the easiest way to transport your gear. All you need to do is roll the bike up the ramp into the cargo area or where the cars are carried. Most of the time, there will be ropes and a railing to secure the bike, and you can always use one of the straps or bungees you have used for your packs. You do not need to worry about someone stealing the bicycle. No one is going to jump into the water and swim away with it. However, you should bring anything valuable or easily stolen with you into the passenger area.

Airplanes

I frequently transport my bicycle by airplane. Unfortunately, this is one of the most complex methods. One issue that is always of concern is damage control. Michael and I endured a bent rim and a bent fork on

It is easy to transport a bike by ferry. Just roll it on board and tie it to a railing.

two separate trips before we switched to hard cases. Admittedly, we took several trips with no damage and I know many people who have never had a problem. Still, I am happy my bicycle is protected.

Whenever you travel by airplane, you will need to make at least one or two adjustments to the bicycle. Most airlines require that you turn the handlebars sideways, remove the pedals (or at least attach them to the inside of the crank arms) and let most of the air out of the tires. To make it less likely that the rims will be damaged, do not let all of the air out of the tires.

Use a hex wrench to loosen the handlebar bolt, located at the top where the handlebars go into the frame of the bike. Turn the handlebars and re-tighten the bolt.

The pedals come off by loosening the pedal spindle from the crank arm. The right pedal loosens in the usual counterclockwise direction. The left pedal has left-hand thread and loosens in a clockwise direction. The most convenient way to transport the pedals is to screw them in again on the *inside* of the crank arms.

Items that are not permanently fastened, such as cycle computers, lights, or packs of any kind, should be removed and placed in a more secure pack or carried on board.

Shipping Boxes

Many airlines will sell you a cardboard box to put the bike into. These boxes tend to be thin and to fall apart quickly. Using them is almost the same as using nothing, except that the boxes are less convenient. If you are not ready financially to make the leap to a hard case, an excellent alternative is to go to a bicycle shop and ask for a shipping box. These are the boxes that manufacturers use to ship new bicycles to the shop. They are sturdy and have inserts and attachments designed to package the bicycle safely. They come in different sizes so be sure you tell them what you will be packing so you will get the right size box. If possible, call ahead of time and ask if someone will show you how to disassemble the bicycle and pack it into the box. You should offer and expect to pay them for their time.

Re-Usable Boxes

There are numerous travel cases available commercially. Personally, I do not see the value of the re-usable corrugated cardboard models. You will do just as well with a shipping box from a shop. The re-usable boxes are much more expensive than anyone will charge you for help with a shipping box.

Permanent Cases

Among the "permanent" cases available, you can find soft- and hard-sided models. These cases are expensive but if you decide to travel often with your bicycle they make sense. Bicycles get banged around by baggage handlers and from shifting cargo en route.

Cases that have handles and wheels can be rolled rather than carried. Some cases hold both the bicycle and the wheels. Others carry only one or the other. There are advantages to having two separate cases. A bicycle is a big item. Any case capable of holding the entire bike without any disassembly may be too big for standard shipping, whether it is part of your luggage or you send it separately. It will also be more difficult to get into your car.

You may have a vehicle large enough to carry it but will you be able to find transportation at your destination? If the case is not too big, it can be carried in a station wagon or a van. Many taxi companies have larger vehicles for people with a lot of luggage. You will probably have to pay a bit extra for the extra baggage.

Michael's Boxes

Michael solved our traveling dilemma by building boxes out of luan plywood. The luan was cut only slightly larger than the bicycle frame. The depth of the box is just a bit wider than the widest part of the bicycle, the rear dropouts. He cut a small wood block to fit into each inside corner and then screwed the pieces together. The corners are reinforced with fiberglass, inside and out. The final step was attaching handles and wheels.

We "sew" the lid onto the box with shock cord. Michael drilled several holes that pass at an angle through both the lid and the box. It takes only two or three minutes to lace the cord through and it gives us a closure that would probably outlast the box itself.

The boxes are constructed to fit the frame's exact dimensions, so that they are as small as possible. This means that we need to take everything off the frame: handlebars, fork, racks, seatpost, pedals and crank arms, rear derailleur, and wheels. This is not as hard as it may seem. All of these attach to the frame with screws, nuts, and bolts. We need an adjustable wrench, pliers, screwdrivers (Phillips and flat head), and a set of hex wrenches.

There is room for gear after we put all of the bike parts in. We use the tent, tarp, and clothes to provide padding. I put clothes into a plastic shopping bag to keep them clean, but still loose enough to squeeze into place around the bicycle.

Higher Education

I have learned more about my bicycle from taking it apart and putting it back together than I have from any other experience. It provides an opportunity to inspect and clean the bicycle and make sure everything is in working order, not only before we go, but also before I start riding when I come home.

Storing the Cases

Finding a place to leave a case is not usually a problem. Check with the airline. Perhaps they have a place where you can store the case at the

Here is Michael's bike broken down and packed in its custom hard case.

airport until your return flight. If you can bicycle from the airport to your destination, you can assemble the bike and load your gear right in the airport and take off from there. The same is true for train and bus stations.

Almost all hotels will hold your case for you if you return for your last night. Since we need to assemble our bikes, we like to start our trip in a hotel so that we have a convenient spot to spread everything out. The same is true on the last day.

If you want to start out in one place and end up in another, it is more difficult. That is a good time to consider the disposable shipping boxes. Keep in mind, though, that you may not be able to find one for your return flight.

Protecting the Bicycle

Regardless of how you ship your bike, be sure it has at least some protection. If you have removed the wheels, try to brace the inside of the fork and the rear stays. You can buy dummy axles to slip in or you can make wood or plastic blocks and tape them on. If you are using airline boxes or no boxes, consider inexpensive foam pipe insulation to slip onto the tubes for protection. Shift the derailleurs to the farthest outside gears. Wrap more delicate parts, such as the derailleurs and the brakes, in newspaper for extra padding. Use duct (cloth) tape or strapping tape to seal the box. And put your name on everything!

Costs

Buses and trains almost always charge extra for bicycles. How much more varies from one company to another, but it is usually not prohibitive. Airlines, on the other hand, usually charge $50 or $60 each way for bicycles, regardless of how you have packed it. I have heard a few innovative ways to conceal the fact that your crate carries a bicycle — from putting a handicapped sticker on it to breaking it down into a couple of boxes. Frankly, I would spend the entire flight worrying that someone was going to discover the truth and ruin my vacation by confiscating either the bike or me, so I play it honestly.

I have found that on most international flights there used to be no charge for the bicycle as long as you have only one other bag. However, there is a rumble that even this has changed.

We usually strap two panniers together with straps and lots of duct tape. Then we have two boxes with the bikes and one bag with the wheels. We carry the rest on the plane. We can get 75 percent of our gear into the bike boxes and the panniers. Each of us carries a handlebar bag and one pannier on board.

You must be vigilant about assuring that airport personnel are informed that your bicycle is flying free. This can be a problem if you must take a domestic flight to reach your international carrier. When you purchase the tickets, request that the record is marked with a statement stating clearly that the bicycles are free. Even if you receive electronic tickets, get something in writing to show when you check in.

Members of the League of American Bicyclists (LAB) and Adventure Cycling can arrange for free air travel for their bicycles under some circumstances. You must use approved travel agents and participating airlines. For LAB members, the free coupons are only available for flights that cost over $200 each way or $300 round trip. The number of airlines that participate is limited in both programs. I have used this service several times and found that although I did not always receive the best fare, the price was still less than I would have paid for a better fare plus the cost of the bicycles.

Many cyclists, including myself, are annoyed that bicycles are singled out for increased charges when other sports equipment, such as golf clubs and skis, are not. The argument the airlines give is that bicycles cannot be sent to the planes on the conveyor belt and so require special handling which golf clubs and skis do not. However, many bicycle cases (including mine) fit on the conveyor without difficulty and they are almost always considered "bicycles," yet the charge still applies.

Shipping by Ground Service

Many cyclotourists are using independent shipping companies to send their bike to their destination. Also, many long-distance bus companies carry freight. In many cases it is cheaper than paying the airlines fee. You may need to send the bicycle as much as ten days before the start of your trip. Add a day or two to the maximum amount time anticipated just to be safe.

This means you also need a place to ship the bicycle to. Most hotels and hostels will be happy to receive your package and hold it for you until you arrive (mark "Hold for guest arriving [date]"). Many campgrounds will as well. This will eliminate the problem of transportation from the airport. Some shipping companies will even pick your box up from your home.

Also consider local bicycle shops. When you ask about receiving the bike, ask how much they charge for assembly. It may be inexpensive and convenient enough to be worth the cost.

If you prefer, bus companies (and possibly railways) will hold your crate at the terminal until you pick it up. Find out the precise procedure and label it "Hold for pick-up" so it will not disappear into the lost luggage labyrinth before you arrive.

Shippers may charge extra for over-size parcels so you can sometimes save by packing your wheels in a separate box. This also means, however, that there are now two chances for lost freight. We spent several hours lolling around Shannon Airport in Ireland waiting for our wheels, which managed to get onto a different flight than our bicycles. However, in some cases it may be necessary if the shipper has a limit on the overall size.

If you decide to use a shipping company, you will need to do at least some disassembly. Many shippers will not take a bicycle unless it is in a sturdy box or case. And of course, you still need to package the bicycle well enough that it is not damaged en route.

Finally, do not let any of the potential difficulties discourage you. While it is a little more work, it is definitely worth it to be able to travel by bicycle.

13.

The Care and Feeding of the Cyclotourist

One of the best parts of a cycling vacation is that you can eat all that you want and not worry about fitting into your clothes. This is especially nice when visiting places known for their cuisine. No need to worry if you should have a second chocolate croissant or pass on the roasted peppers drenched in olive oil. Baklava, Swiss chocolate, go ahead. Enjoy.

Cooking

You can eat every meal in restaurants or you can prepare some or all of your own. Cooking for yourself will save money and it may be necessary if you plan to travel in areas with few tourist amenities. It will also give you greater flexibility. But it does involve some extra gear and effort. You will need to bring pans, dishes, and utensils. If we plan to cook, we bring cups for hot drinks, although some space-minded people use their water bottles for all beverages. A collapsible water container comes in handy if you plan to camp. It will save you the effort of hiking back and forth for cooking and cleaning water.

If you plan to cook your meals, you will need fuel. It is prohibited to carry fuel on an airplane so you will need to obtain it at your destination. For our single burner back pack stove, we use regular automobile gasoline which is almost universally available. Most of the time, white gas, our stove's preferred fuel, is sold in gallon containers, much too big to carry on tour. So we would need to fill our stove and fuel bottle and find a safe place to get rid of the rest. Occasionally, we have been fortunate to find people in large camp grounds who will give us a bit of white gas to fill our stove.

Let's Pack it In

In most campgrounds, water is available. Some remote sites may not have potable water, so you will need to carry it in. In that case, canned foods that only need to be heated are good choices since you will not need separate containers for the water. However, you may still want to carry a large container of water especially if you will be staying more than one day. There are many shapes and sizes of inexpensive collapsible plastic containers that are very convenient to carry empty. Carrying a couple of gallons on your bike can be a major challenge, but it may be necessary. This is one trick you will want to try at home before you leave.

Try freeze-dried foods at home as well. Some of the specialized camping food is close to inedible despite gourmet names like Burgundy Beef or Yankee Pot Roast. Some of the just-add-water foods from the grocery store are not any better. It is depressing to end a long day, camping in the middle of nowhere with a big helping of nasty tasting goo.

I lump the typical sports bars into this category. They are nutritious, small, and lightweight. You can eat them while riding with little hassle and they will not spoil even after a day in your jersey pocket, with sun and sweat attacking them for hours on end. Personally, I would rather carry dried fruit or nuts, or better yet, stop for an ice cream cone. But this is your vacation, you decide.

Serving Suggestions

When Michael and I make casseroles out of whatever we have available, we call it "garbage stew," but it is much tastier than it sounds. For camping, we use quick rice, cous-cous and small pasta or noodles because they take only a little time and fuel to cook. We combine these with just-add-water sauces, dried vegetables, nuts, and fresh vegetables when we can get them. On our last trip, we carried a small bottle of olive oil that made the stew especially good. This made it easy to make a stir fry with fresh or dried vegetables.

There are also a variety of meats that can be used in camping food. Dried meats like pepperoni, hard salami, dried beef or beef jerky work well. There are also canned meats, such as tuna, salmon, ham salad, clams, beef, chicken, and shrimp.

Pasta sauce will not spoil before it is opened, and is tasty and easy to prepare. However, it is packaged in heavy, breakable glass jars. It may be possible to carry some sauce in a plastic bottle if you will be eating it soon. Sometimes you can find pasta sauce in a jar small enough for one meal. It also helps to have a jar of mixed spices, such as Italian spices, curry or other commercially prepared mixtures.

Dried mixes are easy to carry on the bike. To save room in your packs, take them out of the boxes and put them into zippered plastic bags. Tear off directions and put them in the bag too.

Fresh fruits and vegetables will ripen rapidly in the sun. Buy them when they are a bit under-ripe, keep them out of direct sun and plan to eat them soon. Soft foods will squish easily from bouncing and jostling as you ride, so pack them carefully. Putting them in plastic bags will help avoid a mess if they do get squashed.

Sweets like candy, cakes, cookies, and bars make a nice treat and can give an energy boost when you need it. But remember that chocolate melts at fairly low temperatures. Once again, our old friend the zippered plastic bag comes in handy. Chocolate is still good when it is gooey. Cakes and cookies need careful packaging but the crumbs are still tasty if they do downsize.

Camping supply stores sell food tubes. These look like large re-usable toothpaste tubes. They are filled from the bottom where a pin is attached to seal it. To eat the food, you remove the cap from the other end and squeeze. These are great for butter, margarine, peanut butter, and jelly or any smooth spread. Just make sure whatever you put in the bottom is small enough to come out the top.

It is easy to make tea or coffee at your campsite using bags or instant powders. There are several other drinks that come in powdered form. Some are already mixed with sugar or sugarless sweeteners and some you can mix the sugar to your own taste, which is often preferable. I usually find that prepared sweet drinks are too sweet for touring. One of my favorites is powdered lemonade, which is quite tart, mixed to about half strength or less. I then add a teaspoon or so of sugar to decrease the tartness. Be careful if you put anything other than water into your bottles. The environment is perfect for molds and you will need to wash the bottles frequently.

Animal Thieves

In campgrounds, raccoons and other critters have learned that people food tastes better than acorns and berries. They have also learned that taking food away from campers can be as easy as taking candy from a baby. Many state and national parks provide cupboards to keep the critters out. If you do not have that luxury, hang your food in a tree. Put all the food into a pack and tie bungees or straps to the handle. The best technique is to throw the "rope" over a sturdy, high branch and hoist the pack. The pack should hang far enough away from the trunk, low enough from the branch and high enough off the ground that animals cannot reach it.

Raccoons are notorious for their skill and cunning at stealing food, and they eat everything including leather, paper and plastic if it smells like food. They can smell those cookies you brought into the tent with you for a midnight snack. And do not think that your presence will deter them. They will chew their way into your tent, rip open your panniers, and steal the goodies while you sleep.

When Michael and I were young and foolish, we stayed in a lean-to on a popular trail in the Adirondacks. We forgot to put away a bag of pretzels when we went to bed. As soon as it was dark, a raccoon climbed into our lean-to, merrily gorging himself on the pretzels. We

This was our campsite on the north rim of the Grand Canyon. Camping increases your options on a bike tour.

thought that shining our flashlight in his eyes would frighten him off, but he just squinted at us as if to say, "Hey, turn that light off. I'm trying to eat here!"

Michael got up and chased him off, but as soon as he got into his sleeping bag and turned off the flashlight, the raccoon was back. We then had a brilliant idea. "Let's just scatter the pretzels into the woods. The raccoon will eat his fill and then go away and leave us alone."

Well, it worked just that way up until "and leave us alone." He did leave, but not for long. He went to home to collect his family so they could enjoy the feast. The babies were not as quiet as the adults and chirped and squeaked in between bites. We did not get to sleep until the last of the pretzels was consumed.

If park officials catch you feeding raccoons or other wild creatures intentionally, they will read you the riot act, with good reason. Campers who encourage animals to scavenge food from humans do not only turn wild animals into pests. Park rangers can tell you a hundred stories about animals who became sick and died from eating human food, garbage, and food packaging. If they want to eat human food, let them do their own grocery shopping and bake their own cookies.

Building a Fire

If you want to build a fire to cook, for warmth or for atmosphere, please use only existing, approved fire rings. In addition to the risk of starting a larger fire, building a fire in the open leaves an ugly scar that will take a generation to heal. It makes me sad and angry to see the mess left behind by some selfish person who decided that a little personal ambiance justified creating an eyesore for everyone who follows.

Eating Out

It is not necessary to carry a stove to be able to make your own meals. There are many varieties of ready-to-eat food available, including sandwiches, fruit, baked goods, and a host of other possibilities. If you plan to prepare all or many of your meals, you will be much happier with a stove and the options one will give you. However, if you only plan to eat lunches and one or two other meals on your own, you may be fine without one.

Be Prepared

Whether you decide to cook or not, always carry enough food for at least your next meal. If you get hungry where there is no restaurant, having something to munch on will make your day much more enjoyable.

What to Eat, When, and How to Eat It

When you are bicycling all day for a couple of weeks, you will need more water and more calories. Electrolytes, such as sodium and potassium, are needed in higher amounts as well, but most prepared food contains more than enough sodium, and eating fruit will replace the potassium.

Michael and I take vitamins at home and frequently when we tour. Many nutritionists say that a healthy diet will provide all the nutrients that humans need, but that would require having a healthy diet. I am not that careful about my food intake, so I take supplements of the essentials.

Even though you should sample local foods, try to maintain to a diet similar to what you are used to. Radical changes of any kind can make you feel ill. You do not need to eliminate rich foods, but it is best to partake in small amounts spaced throughout the day.

Eat frequently during the day, at least every couple of hours. You are burning up calories as you pedal, and it is best to replace them as you use them rather than in one or two large meals.

Do not put a crimp in your vacation by trying to lose weight. It is possible that you will lose a few pounds, but you will feel better if you eat as much as your body tells you to eat.

If you do not feel like eating you are working too hard. Slow down, take a break or shorten your daily mileage. Losing the desire to eat is one of the symptoms of exhaustion. When I am on a single-day ride with other people, I always hear at least one person say that they cannot eat until after the ride is completed and they have stopped for the day. This is impractical for a multiple day trip. Lower your level of activity to a point where you are comfortable eating as you go.

Staying Hydrated

You will lose water through sweat, more so when it is hot. As with eating, it is better to drink small amounts frequently. Sip continuously as you ride, drinking at least a glass every hour. Some experts recommend two glasses every hour and most certainly you will need more in hot weather. Water is all you need but dilute fruit juices or sports drinks will also provide calories and salts. You will also drink more if the beverage tastes good. At least a couple of sports drinks are available in powdered form, and sometimes I carry some of this if I expect hot weather when I will probably drink more than I eat.

Carry at least two water bottles with you, but do not pass up opportunities to get other drinks. Cold fluids are absorbed faster which gives you an excuse to take the time to stop. Stopping along the way is part of the joy of touring. It affords an opportunity to meet people, savor a view, share impressions with your companions and just generally enjoy the moment while tasting local foods and beverages.

Continue to eat and drink after you have stopped for the day. There is a limit to how quickly your body can absorb food and water. If it is hot or you are working hard, you will need to continue to replenish what you have lost for a few hours after you have put the bicycle to bed.

Table 12-1: Some suggestions for food to carry and eat along the way

◻ Firm fruit such as apples, oranges

◻ Hard breads, such as bagels and Kaiser rolls

◻ Dilute fruit juices (carry in your water bottles)

◻ Sweets, such as cookies and candy (remember, chocolate melts)

◻ Preserved meats (hard salami, dried beef, pepperoni, beef jerky)

◻ Canned meats (tuna, chicken, ham salad, clams, shrimp, salmon, etc.)

◻ Canned fruits

◻ Nuts, trail mixes

◻ Peanut butter and jelly

◻ Bars (breakfast, granola, sports, candy, brownies)

Table 12.2: More suggestions for camping food

◻ All of the above plus:

◻ Pasta, noodles, quick rice, cous-cous (plain or mixes with spices)

◻ Dried vegetables and soups

◻ Just-add-water sauces and foods, such as macaroni and cheese

◻ Canned stews, chili, soups, pasta, and tomato sauce

◻ Powdered drinks

◻ Gatorade, sugar-sweetened and non-sugar kid's drinks, hot chocolate, hot apple cider, powdered milk

◻ Just-add-water pancake and biscuit mixes

◻ Cream soups as sauces

◻ Ultra-pasteurized milk (Needs no refrigeration until it is opened)

◻ Tea bags, coffee bags, or instant coffee

Dealing with Some of the Most Common Health Problems Experienced by Cyclotourists

Digestive Problems

The most common illnesses that travelers face involve the digestive system. "Montezuma's revenge" is the scourge of tourists the world over. This relatively mild form of diarrhea is caused by microorganisms in the local water that are not found in your water at home. It is more likely to be a problem in countries with less processing and quality control of tap water. If in doubt, buy bottled water, boil water before you drink it, or drink only processed beverages, such as soda. Fruit juices that are processed locally may be worse than the tap water. Local fruit should be washed thoroughly or avoided. Fruits that must be peeled are usually safe because the offending microbes are on the surface. Thorough washing may also help.

The strongest over-the-counter anti-diarrheal drugs are synthetic narcotics, such as Immodium, generic name loperamide. (By the way, they do not cause the same pain-killing or mood altering effects as true narcotics and they are not addictive.) These are too harsh for some people and medications such as Kaopectate may be a better choice. It is not as fast or as sure, but it does not cause back-lash constipation cramps. If you can take the synthetic narcotics without problems, they are the best and you should be feeling fine the next day if not in an hour or two. Both kinds of medications are available in tablets.

Remember, though, that diarrhea dehydrates the body very quickly and very thoroughly. If the problem continues for more than a couple of hours, I recommend spending a second day either resting or at least at a lower level of exertion so that you will have time to reabsorb fluids.

Constipation

Constipation is the flip side of the coin. It is not local microbial flora and fauna that is the culprit here, but rather a drastic change of diet. Most processed "convenience" foods lack fiber. Frequently, this kind of food is the mainstay of travelers especially campers. The best way to prevent such a problem is to continue to get fruit and fiber in your diet. Also, keeping well-hydrated will help. There are over-the-counter drugs for this, but they can be harsh as well. Unless you have a chronic problem with this, I would recommend trying to improve your diet as a solution.

Fatigue

Finding yourself too tired to continue can be caused by many conditions. Heat, overexertion, cold, rain, not eating enough, not replacing lost salts, low blood sugar, and dehydration are all possible culprits. Which one is more likely to occur depends on you and your tour. All of these are easily avoidable but sometimes you may find yourself pushing too hard. If you are unaware of the potential problems, or if you plan a tour that is too difficult or ambitious, it is more likely that you will go over your limits.

Dehydration

Dehydration is the most common problem among athletes in general. Sweat is one of the body's best mechanism for dissipating heat. When the air is dry, keeping cool is easier because the sweat evaporates quickly. Also, as you move the bicycle, the breeze you create will help evaporate skin moisture. However, you may not realize how much moisture you have lost.

Experts say you need at least one to two glasses of water an hour while you are exercising. That amount increases with the temperature and your level of exertion. The best drinks are plain water or drinks with around six percent sugar, about half as much as soda. Sports drinks provide calories and salts at this level and are good beverage choices. However, they are not necessary as long as you continue to eat normally.

Prevention: Drink before you are thirsty, drink small amounts frequently, and drink at least one to two glasses per hour. Continue to drink fluids for a few hours after you have stopped for the day because it is possible to lose water faster than you can re-absorb it especially in hot weather.

Signs and symptoms: Headache, fatigue, dry mouth, thirst. Urination is less frequent than normal or absent and the urine is dark.

As dehydration worsens, symptoms include dizziness, confusion, low blood pressure and an increase in heart rate and breathing. At this level, dehydration can be fatal if it is untreated

Treatment: Drink two or three glasses of fluids a sip at a time and rest. When urination frequency and color are normal, you will be able to continue at a normal pace. You should feel fine the next day, but if you do not, take it easy another day and drink at least two glasses an hour.

Rest, eat, and drink adequately if you start to feel fatigued. You'll be back on the road in no time.

Hyperthermia

Excessive heat can increase the risk of dehydration, and dehydration increases the risk of heat exhaustion. However, they are two separate problems and you can suffer from heat exhaustion even if you are fully hydrated.

While sweating is an efficient way of cooling off in most situations, when it is very hot, humid or you are working hard, it does not matter how much you drink, you are going to get hot and tired. If you are a snow bunny who has traveled to the tropics to escape your local winter, you will not be used to the heat, which will increase the likelihood of getting heat exhaustion.

Prevention: Once again, this is completely avoidable if you use common sense and do not set a rigid schedule. Avoid riding in the hottest times of the day, or at least slow down and make frequent stops. Take rest breaks in the shade. Drink at least two glasses of water per hour and continue to eat normally. Heat exhaustion can be reversed easily and quickly if you stop and rest, preferably out of the sun.

Do not drink alcohol, caffeine or hot drinks on a hot day. Do not take drugs that are fever reducers, including aspirin, acetaminophen and ibuprofen. If you get a headache or your muscles start bugging you, stop and rest rather than tossing back an aspirin or two.

Signs and symptoms: Headache, fatigue, cold clammy skin, increased pulse rate and breathing rate, confusion, dizziness, shivering or goose flesh. Stop and rest before symptoms worsen.

As heat exhaustion increases, the skin becomes hot and dry. Nausea, weak pulse, dilated pupils, disorientation and fainting are signs of heat stroke which is life-threatening. At this point, the body's ability to maintain the correct temperature is seriously compromised. Seek immediate emergency medical care.

Treatment: Stop cycling, get out of the sun, drink water or fluids with a small amount of sugar. Dilute fruit juices are ideal. If you can go into an air-conditioned building, that is great. If you can drink cold water, do so. Fan yourself to increase the rate of cooling.

Muscle Cramps

Exhaustion can also cause muscle cramps especially in the legs. Deciding exactly which form of exhaustion has caused the cramps may be difficult since so many of these conditions affect each other. Muscle cramps can be caused by lack of glucose, calcium or salt especially potassium, excess heat, dehydration, and over-use. Take your pick, the treatment for all of them is rest, eat, and drink.

Prevention: Eat, drink, rest frequently.

Signs and Symptoms: Muscle cramps, fatigue

Treatment: Rest, massage, eat, and drink (not too hard to take, eh?)

Hypothermia

Since most of us prefer to take our vacations in places with warm temperatures, hypothermia is not usually a great risk to the cyclotourist. However, it does not have to be extremely cold to get hypothermia. Most cases of hypothermia occur between 30 and 60 degrees F (–1 to 16 degrees C). Especially with temperatures in the 40's and 50's (5 to 15 degrees C) people are not as careful as they are at lower temps.

Cycling will keep you warm, but you will cool off quickly when you stop. The risk increases if someone is ill, dehydrated, exhausted or wet. A body can cool down 25 times faster in water than in air at the same temperature. The wind chill factor also plays a role. Strong wind will cool you by increasing the evaporation of sweat and sweeping your body heat away more quickly.

Prevention: Be sure you have warm, dry clothes to put on at the end of the day. When you stop for breaks along the way, put on a jacket and other clothing as needed. When it is cold and windy, cover as much of your skin as possible. Even lightweight clothing will help reduce heat loss. Do not forget your face.

Just as evaporation of sweat cools the body, evaporation of the moist air in your lungs also contributes to as much as a third of heat loss. Covering your mouth and nose with even a light cloth will reduce heat loss.

Keep eating and drinking. You need calories to keep your body temperature up. Drink warm fluids like soup or herbal teas. Do not drink alcohol or caffeinated drinks.

Signs and Symptoms: Shivering, poor muscle coordination, confusion, slow pulse, fatigue, slurred speech.

Treatment: Put on more clothing. Stop at the next place with heat or at least is out of the wind. Drink warm liquids. Quit riding for the day as soon as you can. If you can stay indoors, do so. If not, get into your sleeping bag, preferably with another person. If you must continue riding, do not push as exhaustion can make the situation worse. Stay shielded from the wind. Confusion is an early symptom so watch each other.

General Advice

Regardless of what type of exhaustion we are discussing, among the first signs are headache, fatigue and loss of appetite. Listen to your body. Do not set a rigid schedule. After you have treated the immediate situation, rest. Go more slowly, take a shorter day, take a day off, take it easy until you feel completely better. Give your body a chance to get back to normal before picking up the pace again.

Other common symptoms are poor judgment and confusion. Watch each other. If someone complains of fatigue, listen. As the exhaustion increases, it may make the affected person unable to judge correctly how he or she is doing.

Do not reach for the caffeine and ibuprofen. These can make you feel better than you actually are. Reach for your water bottle and a sandwich instead.

Taking Care of Your Knees

To help save your knees from unnecessary pain, rotate the pedals at a faster speed in a lower gear. The speed that you turn your pedals is called cadence or spinning. You want to keep a regular cadence of around 80 pedal turns per minute. Pedaling at a slower rate but with more pressure per turn will be harder on your knees. Use all of your gears and shift frequently as the terrain changes.

Knee pain can also be caused by improper saddle adjustment. If the front of your knees hurt, try raising the saddle. If it is the back of your knee that is the problem, lower the saddle. For pain on the outside of the knee, turn your toes out more. For the inside, try turning your toes inward a bit. You can do this even if you use cleats. The cleat itself, the part on the bottom of your shoe, is adjustable. Use a hex wrench to loosen the cleat a bit, then rotate the cleat a small amount in the correct direction and retighten the cleat. Some kinds of cleats allow for more "float" than others.

Numbness and Tingling in Feet and Hands

When you support yourself by holding onto the handlebars, you are pressing on nerves in the palm of your hand. The longer you ride, the more irritated the nerves get and the more likely you are to feel tingling, numbness, or "electric shock" in your hands. Moving your hands to different positions frequently will help but may not be enough. Use more padding on either your gloves or the handlebars. Keep in mind that you do not want so much padding that you are uncomfortable with the reach.

You can also try tipping your saddle up a bit. You may be sliding off the saddle and putting more pressure than necessary on your hands. However, if this is at all uncomfortable on your derriere, try something else. You do not want to give up one problem for another. Also try raising your handlebars, moving your saddle forward or possibly buying a shorter stem.

If you have straight handlebars, get bar ends for them. These will give you to more hand positions. If you have drop handlebars, change position by using the drops, the top bar and the brake hoods (the tops of the brake mounts).

Problems with your feet are usually due to your shoes. Some considerations for a good pair of shoes were discussed in Chapter 8. Make sure your shoes are not too small or too narrow. Road cycling shoes are frequently narrow in the forefoot. Mountain bike shoes are sometimes better. Mountain bike shoes are also better for touring because they are easier to walk in.

However, mountain bike shoes do not always have as stiff a sole as road bike shoes. The stiffness helps spread the pressure of the pedal so that it is not concentrated on the ball of the foot. This is especially important if you use cleats where your foot is attached to the pedal in one small area.

If the problem continues, get off the bike more frequently and shorten the number of miles you do each day. Rest is the answer to many, many problems.

A Pain in the... Saddle

If your saddle is not comfortable, first try adjusting it. You can change the tilt, the height, and the distance from the handlebars. If adjustment does not work, consider a gel pad that fits over the saddle. If that does not help, get a new one. If you cannot replace the saddle right now, get off the bicycle for a few minutes every hour to reduce the insult to your derriere.

Especially for women, be sure you make frequent pit stops because "holding it" will increase saddle irritation.

Chafe is greatly reduced by wearing cycling shorts, with no underwear. If you do not have them with you, stopping more frequently will help as will shortening the number of miles per day. Moist skin is more likely to chafe than dry skin. Getting off the bike for a bit will allow the parts of your shorts and bottom that contact the saddle to dry. You can also use petroleum jelly or other moisturizers to reduce the chafe. Your buns take a lot of abuse on a long tour. It pays to keep them happy.

"Road Rash"

The most common injury from a fall is scraped skin and bruises, called "road rash." While this is not serious, it can be painful. Clean the area and apply neosporin or another antibacterial cream. Keep the area covered if you can. This will keep it cleaner and will also prevent drying and cracking.

If you take a fall, do not jump up immediately. First orient yourself and take inventory to see if everything is OK. Anything feel particularly painful? Can you move easily? If you have any of the following symptoms, seek emergency medical help: numbness, nausea, blurred vision, unclear memory of the fall, sharp or intense pain, profuse bleeding, dizziness or confusion.

Check the bike carefully before you head off again. You may need to adjust the brakes, derailleur, handlebars or saddle. Also look for bent wheels, frame or other signs of structural damage. You may need to hitch a ride on a passing pick-up truck or ask a motorist to call for help.

Miscellany

Take a few small bandages for blisters or small cuts. I also pack hydrocortisone cream which will help for poison ivy or other skin irritations. Petroleum jelly will help keep chafe from getting worse. It also is great for removing grease.

Security

Unfortunately theft and security issues need to be addressed. The good news is that a little attention will prevent most problems. You should always bring a lock with you.

U-shaped locks are the hardest to cut by would-be thieves and are the locks of choice if weight is less a consideration than security. The best way to use one is to remove your front wheel and lean it against the rear wheel. Pass the U through both wheels, the frame (seatstays or rear stays), and onto some strong fixed structure, like a bike rack or a sign post. If you intend to leave your bike out of your sight for any length of time in an area even the slightest bit suspicious, you may need to carry a lock like this on your tour. However, they are heavy, and if you can get away with something smaller and lighter, do so.

A strong cable and strong padlock or combination lock works for most cyclotourists. A cable that is long enough to loop through both wheels and the frame without removing the front wheel is the most convenient. It also gives you more room if you cannot find a thin structure to lock to.

Using Bicycle Racks

When you lock your bicycle to a bicycle rack, do not use up more than your share of space. Give the next guy a place to lock up, too.

Do not create a hazard. Never block pedestrian pathways with your locked bike. Do not lock your bike to a handrail unless you can do so without obstructing pedestrians. Handrails are meant to be used by those who have difficulty walking. If your bike is in the way you will make their progress even more difficult.

We carried freeze-dried food to Iceland because there were no services for hundreds of miles on this road.

Safe Overnight Storage

I feel much safer if the hotel allows me to bring my bike into my room. If this is not allowed, talk to the desk staff and find a safe place where you can lock it and it will be watched by hotel staff. I have never had to leave my bike on the street when I stayed at a hotel.

Camp Security

Lock your bicycle in campgrounds. If you have a cable, you may be able to lock it to something permanently placed. A disabled bicycle is much less likely to be targeted than one that can be easily removed. Incapacitating the bike is as simple of putting the lock through both the frame and one of the wheels. If you have room in your tent, remove one of the wheels and take it inside. If you put the bike close to the tent, you are also more likely to hear someone fiddling with it and chase them away.

Other than the pretzel-craving raccoons, I have only had unfriendly visitors during the night on one occasion. We stopped for the night in a sugar cane field in Cuba. The land is collective so no one feels possessive or considers trespassing a problem. It was a lovely, moonless night with a good breeze keeping the mosquitoes away. We cooked dinner and piled most of our gear right at the entrance to the tent. There was not a single cloud in the sky so we left our rain fly off. The tent is mostly netting, so we get a good view of the sky (and in this case, the surrounding sugar cane). Shortly after we got into the sleeping bags, Michael thought he saw a head above the cane on the right side. He got up, called out, shone the flash light, but saw nothing. He convinced himself that he had imagined it and we went back to sleep.

I am a light sleeper, and a couple of hours later I "felt" something was amiss. I opened my eyes to see a figure crouched in front of the tent. I sat up and he bolted away into the cane. I woke Michael and we got out of the tent to try to find the guy. Nothing. We got back into the tent, wary and tense. Over the next hour, I dozed on and off a bit, but Michael stayed awake. Suddenly he started shouting, "Hey! You! Scram!" Once again we were both out of the tent, looking. Michael saw him run to the edge of the cane and stop so he started talking to him in broken Spanish.

"Who are you? Why are you bothering us? We need to sleep. Do we need to go? If you will not go then we need to go."

We could see the lights of a work crew several rows away from us and thought about running over. Instead, we started packing our stuff, figuring that we were not going to get any sleep here so we should just leave. We were not happy about it because it was pitch black and we were afraid we would miss something. Michael continued to talk to the guy and I guess we were making a fair amount of noise shuffling things around.

Suddenly the guy spoke. "Via tranquilla!" in an urgent whisper. "Be quiet!"

Michael spoke even louder. "If you will not leave, we must. We need to sleep. Will you go away? Will you let us sleep? OK?"

"OK," came the voice and he started walking toward the work crew.

We stayed up a while longer, but figured he had been with the work crew and was worried about them finding out he was hassling us. Anyway, we finally got some sleep but woke early and left as soon as we could. I would rather have raccoons. On the other hand, the Cuban got nothing and the raccoons ate our pretzels.

Theft Insurance

Write down the bicycle's serial number and keep it with you when you must leave the bike. Also, write a note saying, "This Bicycle Was Stolen." Include your name, address, phone number, and the bicycle serial number and push the note down the seat tube. If an honest person or a bike shop buys the bike from the thief, you may be able to get the bike back.

Women on Their Own

Many women feel insecure about traveling alone. Since women may be more likely to become targets for crime than men, it is a good policy to be wary. Be careful about discussing your specific route plans with strangers. Try to ask uniformed personnel, such as police officers for directions, rather than unknown people. If you wish to travel with people you meet, stick to groups rather than a single individual.

Money on the Road

We have already talked about money in its various forms. Now we'll consider what to do with it as you travel. I will repeat that you should be cautious with your cash. You may find it necessary or most convenient to carry a large sum, but store it in separate places. Keep a small amount readily available for purchases and find a secure spot for the rest. Some people carry a pouch that slips under their clothes: shirt, waistband, socks, etc. This will help prevent pickpockets, but it is common enough that thieves know to look for it. We have a small pocket sewn into the bottom inside of one of our panniers. We keep extra money and plane tickets there.

Pickpockets are a problem wherever tourists gather. You can avoid them by being watchful. The most common technique is to create a diversion. Then a second accomplice picks your pocket when you are distracted. First, do not let anyone you do not know touch you. They can't get your money if they can't touch you. Placing your money on the front of your body helps you keep track of it. Wear your fanny pack on your stomach and do not put your wallet into your back pocket. Sling your shoulder bag over your neck and shoulder to make it harder for a thief to slip off. Keep the bag itself on your chest, not your back.

Avoid backpacks. We witnessed what we believe to have been a theft-in-progress in Istanbul. Two men were standing at a T-shirt stall. One man had his hand behind the other, very gingerly pulling on the zipper of the other's backpack.

Michael asked the victim, "Is this guy a friend of yours?" He nodded. Michael said, "So it's all right that he has his hand in your backpack?"

The backpack wearer looked with shock at his buddy who wore a very guilty look on his face. We walked away, having done our civic duty so we do not know the outcome. We assume the friendship did not last long.

Another instructive story took place in Rome. A friend had a shoulder bag with all her money, cards, passport, and plane tickets. She was approached by an old woman dressed in rags carrying a baby. The woman put an arm on Celia's shoulder, not the one with the strap, and began begging for money "por la bambina."

Celia quickly extracted herself, only to discover that her bag had been emptied of all its valuable contents. She figured that the baby was actually tied on, one arm of the coat tied to the bundle. The beggar put one hand on the left shoulder to distract Celia while the other hand, under the baby, reached into the bag over Celia's right shoulder and deftly pulled out wallet and other papers. Again, avoid allowing anyone to touch you. In a crowd, pull your belongings to your chest and put your hands over them.

Dealing With Dogs

A dog that is running free is the nemesis of many cyclists. While actual bites are very rare, they have certainly frightened quite a few of us. My primary concern is that the dog does not cause me to lose control of the bike and take a fall.

The best technique for dealing with them is to shout, "Sit!" A dog with any training at all is likely to know this command and most will automatically comply or at least pause to think about it. By the time they figure out that they were conned, you will be long gone. If "Sit" does not work, try "No!" with equal force. You may want to add these commands to your list of words to learn in the local language if you do not already know them. Most dogs are territorial and will leave you alone once you have passed their boundary.

Some people feel more comfortable stopping and dismounting. The idea here is that the dog is only interested in the chase. If you stop playing the game, he will lose interest and go home. If you are afraid of a fall, this may be the best approach.

Some folks advice spraying dogs with your water bottle, pepper spray or hitting them with your frame pump. I have never tried this. First of all, I want to be in complete control of the bicycle, with both hands on the handlebars, if I am trying to out-maneuver a dog. In most cases it would take longer to get out my "weapon" than to ride out of the dog's territory. I have heard stories about pepper spray having no effect on the dog but lingering in the air as the next rider comes along. At that point an angry companion will be a bigger threat than the dog

There is an ultrasonic device available that emits a loud blast audible to dogs and many other animals, but not humans. This is supposed to stop the animal in its tracks. I have not heard of anyone using it on raccoons, but the people I know who have tried it on dogs say it works very well. For now, however, I feel comfortable shouting "Bad dog. Go home!" and pedaling as fast as I can.

I have had only two memorable encounters with dogs. In Ireland, Michael was ahead of me on a country lane. His passage woke an old Cocker Spaniel who was snoozing in the bushes right next to the road. The startled dog began to cross the road, keeping her eyes glued to Michael. I was too close to avoid her and she bumped into my front wheel. Even more frightened now, she started yelping and rushed home. Michael and I rode to the house and arrived as the owners were coming outside to see what the noise was about. I was so upset that I might have hurt the dog that I was practically in tears. The dog woofed at me as she cowered behind her mistress. The owners assured me that the dog was fine. Yes, she was limping but she always limped because she had arthritis and she was also a bit deaf, which is probably why we took her by surprise, and would we like to come in for a cup of tea?

The second dog incident was in Turkey, where there are lots of cats and dogs that seem to belong to everyone and no one. Most of them are well fed and quite friendly. We were climbing up a long hill on a hot day, when a mutt decided to join us on our journey. We tried to shoo him back home but he was determined to go bicycle touring. He followed us for a mile or so before we crested the hill and started down. He could not keep up with us, so with a wistful sigh for unrequited adventures and unfulfilled quests, he turned around and went home.

Bathing on Tour

If you decide to stay in hotels every night, you will not have to worry about where you will get your next hot shower. You can wash clothes in the sink using a bit of shampoo. Use your straps and bungees as a clothesline if there is not enough towel bar space. If the air is warm and dry, your clothes will probably be dry by morning. If they are not, you can strap them onto your packs so that they can dry as you cycle.

If you will be camping, there are many options. I bring a bottle of shampoo, sealed in a zippered plastic bag, to use for all cleaning. We use it as dish soap, clothing detergent, hand-and-body soap, and even as shampoo. A cotton bandanna works well as a wash cloth for you or your dishes. If you are planning to cook, consider bringing some kind of scrubbing sponge.

Many campgrounds have shower facilities but many do not. Even those that do may be crowded, in poor condition or expensive, and you may want to be prepared to bathe at your tent site instead. In this case, I take a "bird bath" by washing the most offensive spots with a bandanna and soap and take a shower at the next facility.

I have heard a suggestion to use your backpack water container as a small shower by tying it to a tree branch or something else above your head. Some people do the same thing with a plastic collapsible water container.

If you find that there is no private place for your bath or shower, bathe in your swimsuit. We have taken showers at beaches and outdoor public pools in our cycling clothes. The laundry gets done at the same time.

Local Holidays

Local holidays can be part of the fun or can be a serious nuisance depending on how much you know ahead of time. A good guide book will tell you about the major regularly occurring holidays. Keep an eye out for local events advertised on billboards, discussed on television or written about in newspapers. You are traveling at a slow enough pace that you can make inquiries when you are quite close to the event. Find out if local overnight accommodations are likely to be scarce. If they will, call around before you arrive. You can get help from a tourist facility, a hotel in another town, even at grocery stores or other shops.

On my first trip to Ireland, I arrived in Tralee during Easter week, when many school students take holidays. It took many calls, but I found a room. A sympathetic manager for a tiny hotel asked other travelers if they would mind sharing their room with me. We split the cost of the room for two people among the three of us and everyone was happy.

In San Francisco we arrived ahead of schedule. It was a Sunday night outside the tourist season, and we figured there would be no problem finding a room. Wrong! It seemed like every room in a ten mile radius was booked, but with persistent telephoning, each time asking for a suggestion of whom to call next, we found a room in a hostel, close to downtown.

Do not lose hope, someone will put you up. It may be in a private home, it may be for more money than you think is fair, it may not be the best digs in the world, but you will not sleep in a stairway unless that is where you want to be.

You Can't Take It With You

When your tour is coming to an end, begin getting rid of your coins. You will not be able to exchange them. You will be able to exchange your bills, but there will be a fee in that direction as well so you will be charged twice for the exchange. Time your money usage to leave you with as little local currency as possible at the end of the trip. We spend the last of our currency in the airport buying snacks or magazines and newspapers. Most international airports will also accept your home currency so it is a good way to get your wallet back to its native state.

14.

The Responsible Traveler

Traveling to places where people have a different culture from yours is enlightening both for you and for the people you meet. When you travel, you are a guest in someone else's home and you have a responsibility to be courteous to your hosts. The good news is that meeting this responsibility is a great way to get the most pleasure from your trip. It will also leave a positive image of you and your culture.

Sometimes tourists think that because they are spending money, they are doing the entire community a service and everyone they encounter should be grateful for their presence. This attitude is arrogant and not conducive to friendly relations in the first place, but it is also not accurate. Tourism can provide excellent opportunities for the people who live in the area. It can bring in money and elevate the standard of living. Tourism can help promote understanding and goodwill for both tourists and the local population.

Unfortunately, tourism can also damage a culture by reducing religions and beliefs to tourist attractions, polluting resources, overdeveloping areas, increasing crime, and diminishing self-respect by exposure to demeaning tourists. In some extreme situations, the best that the country has to offer may be limited to wealthy tourists and out of reach of people who live there.

If you begin your trip with sensitivity, courtesy, and respect, intending to learn as much as you can from your hosts, you will have a positive experience and will leave positive impressions behind you.

Look at the situation from the perspective of the locals. Think about how you would feel if your situations were reversed. You have no choice but to bring your own culture with you when you travel, however, the best way to anger the locals is to imply directly or indirectly that your culture is superior to theirs.

Some travelers think that they should avoid looking like a tourist. They do not want to appear lost or confused. They try to give the appearance that they are more familiar with the local situation than they really are. This can backfire and you may find yourself even more lost and confused. There is nothing wrong with being unfamiliar with the local situation and there is nothing wrong with admitting it. Besides, acting like a know-it-all can also be irritating and people love to see pompous fools fall on their faces. Appearing just a bit self-effacing will go a long way toward gaining the goodwill of those around you.

Read before you travel. The more you understand the place you are visiting, the less likely you are to offend unintentionally. A good guidebook will tell you about acceptable local dress and behavior. Cyclist's clothing is not acceptable attire in some cultures, so you may have to adapt. While you are cycling, people are less likely to find tight-fitting, revealing cycling clothes out of place. However, they are inappropriate in formal settings from places of worship to many restaurants. Michael and I keep our wind jackets and pants handy and put them on before we go into places where shorts and T-shirts may be in bad taste.

Try to avoid putting up barriers between you and the place you are visiting. By bicycling, you will be much closer to the local culture than if you were in a car or on a tour bus. The low speed and openness of a bike tour make it much more likely that you will interact with the residents. Traveling alone or in a small group, it is much more likely that locals will approach you. These encounters are among the best memories that you will have of your trip. We have received armloads of fresh oranges and grapefruit from Puerto Rican farmers, mangoes and coconuts in Cuba, offers of lunch in Italy, tea and cookies in Ireland, and friendly and helpful advice wherever we travel.

Some activities that tourists pursue are damaging to the local conditions. For example, airplane flights over the Grand Canyon are spectacular and very popular, but they create pollution and noise that has a deleterious effect on plants and animals in the area, not to mention annoying tourists on the ground.

Avoid activities such as feeding wildlife, anything that pollutes, and using valuable resources negligently. Do not use public grounds as toilets. Even in the wilderness, bury solid waste and do not pollute waterways. If water is scarce, use it sparingly.

Be careful where you cycle. One person walking through fragile wildlands may make little or no impact. But when you increase the number of people or the intensity of use, the damage may be permanent. Stay on the paths or trails if you are bicycling on unpaved surfaces. Do not cut down plants to pitch your tent and do not leave trash or garbage behind. If you plan to cook, bring a camping stove. Fire scars take many, many years to heal. Leave the land as it was before you arrived.

Bicycles and camping gear get dirty. It takes care and attention to keep dirt, grease and oil from getting on furniture and walls. Put the bike on top of the ground tarp, plastic trash bags or ask the hotel staff for some old newspapers. Be especially careful if you work on the bike during your stay. Tires make a mark with very little effort, but fortunately they are easy to wipe off. You should be the one to do this, not the housekeeping staff.

This is important for all of us. If one of us makes a mess and the management is annoyed, the next cyclist will get the brunt of the anger. Do not be the last straw that caused management to turn away every cyclist who follows.

If possible, spend your money on local enterprises. Some tourist facilities are run by people who don't come from the local area. These facilities use up local resources and don't put anything back into the community. Buying food from local groceries, staying at locally owned hotels and buying souvenirs that are made in the area will help your vacation spot remain a healthy community.

Learning about history and culture is part of the joy of touring. This Celtic cross is in County Sligo, Ireland.

Coping with a Foreign Language

Many years ago I heard a story about an American woman on one of those one-major-city-per-day tours. The woman went shopping on her own in every city instead of going on the tour bus with the other tourists. She spoke only English and developed the technique of walking into a shop and saying in a loud voice, "Does anyone here speak English?" She found a willing interpreter in every city until the last day. After calling out her usual request, everyone just stared at her. She repeated her request and a cashier said quietly, "Madam, this is London."

Not knowing where you are or what language is being spoken will always create a problem, but for the rest of us there are pocket dictionaries and traveler's phrase books. I am almost fluent in English but that is the only language I speak beyond a three-year-old's level. I have left countless amusing stories behind me, many that I have not heard myself. Still, I have enjoyed trips to many countries and even made friends in countries where English is not used. Hand gestures, sketches, hieroglyphics, and pointing to words and phrases in your book will see you through almost every situation.

Whenever you want to speak to someone, always begin by saying "hello" in the native tongue. Even if your next sentence is in your language, at least you have acknowledged the local language.

Even if you must ask in your own language, your next phrase should be "Do you speak (insert language here)?" Those of us who speak English as a first language have it easy in that in many countries, nearly everyone has studied at least a little English. However, it is still rude to begin with that assumption.

The other absolutely essential word to learn is "thanks." As a traveler, unfamiliar with the area, you will need the good graces and assistance of many people along the way. Knowing how to say "thank you" is another way of acknowledging that you are a foreigner and they are being gracious hosts.

I also recommend learning the words for "good by," "please," and "excuse me." These are also expressions that acknowledge your own language deficit and are polite in all cases.

Just because your waiter knows the word for "chicken" in six major languages does not mean that he is fluent in them. People who work with tourists may only learn the important words and phrases for their jobs. Speak slowly at first, using common words and uncomplicated sentences. Watch and listen to their responses and go from there. As the conversation progresses you can determine how fluent your new friend is and adjust you own speech as needed.

If the people to whom you are speaking do not understand, do not get angry. You may only be tired and frustrated, and not angry at them, but it may look that way. Being polite, even apologetic, goes a long way toward building goodwill and gaining sympathy for your situation. If you attempt to stumble through a phrase book, even if it means pointing to the phrases, you will almost always receive a warm response. And of course, not speaking a second language does not make a person stupid or uneducated, whether they work for the tourist industry or not.

Do not worry that you will enter some dangerous situation because you are not fluent in the native language. It can be frustrating at times, but you will still have your common sense, and that will be your best protection in any situation. "We would like a room" is "Quisieramos una habitacion" in Spanish. When we arrived at one hotel, I was so hot and tired that there was no way my mouth would wrap around "quisieramos." After a couple of incoherent attempts, I settled on "Hay una habitacion?" "Is there a room?" One way or another these things work themselves out.

Most of our "failures to communicate" result in funny, not scary stories. In Iceland, everyone studies English for a few years in school. We still wanted to attempt Icelandic for the sake of being polite, even though it is very different from anything we have ever heard and we were quite atrocious with it. Michael decided to order an ice cream cone in Icelandic, using the word for big or so he hoped. The waitress thought we were German and gave us a very patient lecture on the different words for big and small in English complete with hand gestures.

Table 14-1: Recommended words and phrases

◻ hello (essential)

◻ thank you (essential)

◻ good-bye (strongly recommended)

◻ please (strongly recommended)

◻ excuse me or I'm sorry (strongly recommended)

◻ yes

◻ no

◻ you're welcome

◻ do you speak English?

◻ I understand

- I don't understand
- I want or I would like
- where?
- when?
- how much?
- for how long?
- hotel
- camping
- hostel
- restaurant
- grocery store
- water
- food
- beverages
- toilet
- bicycle
- repairs

Photography

Be cautious about photographing strangers. People are not scenery. You may think you are paying them a compliment, but they may feel that you find them odd or funny. This is especially true of people whose clothing or behavior is governed by religious or cultural beliefs. Remember also that some religions oppose photography of people.

Always ask before you snap the shutter, don't insult people by offering them money and always say "thank you" in the native language. If folks decline, be polite and back down immediately. You may find willing partners who request that you mail them a copy of the photo. Doing this is fun and stretches your trip for a little bit after you get home.

There are usually established rules about any recording of indoor performances, but in most cases you can be comfortable photographing outdoor performances. In this case, the performers may appreciate a tip. Religious performances, of course, are an exception. If doubt, leave your camera in its bag.

Exotic Travel

There are many parts of the world where tourists and touring facilities are rare. The rewards of travel to these places can be great. You can learn first-hand about people who are very different from yourself, perhaps also learning how much you are alike. In Cuba, we drew a crowd everywhere we went. People use bicycles as their primary mode of transportation but not as cyclotourists. Someone would catch up to us and ride next to Michael for a few minutes, staring at our exotic bikes, and then start up a conversation. Wherever we stopped, people gathered to look and ask questions. Kids ran after us as we pedaled by their schools. We were celebrities in a small town where we happened to meet the English teacher who asked us to speak at his class. You will not get that kind of reception in Rome.

However, the more remote the destination, the more self-sufficient you must be. We carried several meals of freeze- dried food

If you practice "freelance camping," leave your campsite exactly the way you found it.

and a hand-pumped water filter to Cuba. We had a tent and sleeping bags and one night we camped in the middle of a sugar cane field. The unexpected is to be expected and you must be willing and able to deal with whatever comes your way even if it means making a big change in your plans. Flexibility is your greatest asset.

You may be able to find companies that offer guided bicycle tours to some exotic locales. The so-called Ecotourism market is expanding and there are companies that will take you to almost any region of the earth. As with any commercial group, do your homework first to assure yourself that they are experienced and competent. The company presumably will attend to all necessary arrangements for food and overnight accommodation which may be rustic or even primitive. Usually very remote areas do not have any tourist facilities and arrangements are made with local groups and choices are few. Michael likes to say that Ecotourism is a way to charge clients more for fewer services. But in many of these places you will have experiences that cannot be had anywhere else on earth.

While you are more likely to be uncomfortable than unsafe, there are some situations that may even be dangerous. The year I wrote this book, several tourists were killed in Uganda by rebel soldiers. This, of course, is extremely unlikely, but do not assume that being on a tour, alone or with a group, exempts you from local problems. Find out enough about your destination ahead of time to be sure you will have what you need to enjoy yourself.

You are the most important factor in determining how much you will enjoy your tour. Be honest with yourself about your expectation and your abilities, be open to new and different experiences, slow down and take in as much as you can — have a great trip!

Appendix

Suggestions for More Information

Publishers

Lonely Planet Travel Survival Kit
Lonely Planet Publications, PO Box
617, Hawthorne, Victoria
3122 Australia. Tel 03 9819 1877
Fax 03 9819 6459
talk2us@lonely planet.com.au
http://www.lonelyplanet.com.au.
LP has general travel guides, walking
guides and are now producing bicycle
guides, which will be worth a look

Eyewitness Travel Guides by DK
Publishing Inc.
95 Madison Ave., NY NY 10016
These guides have lots of detailed
information about culture, history and
places of interest

Falcon Press
PO Box 1718, Helena MT 59624
Tel 800-582-2665
Falcon Scenic Drive books are very
helpful when planning a bike tour.

The Mountaineers
1001 SW Klickitat Way, Seattle WA
98134
There are many specific destination
books as well as how-to guides for out
door recreation

Bicycle Books / MBI Publishers
PO Box 1, Osceola WI 54020
This is a good source for bicycle
how-to books, including repair and
maintenance manuals

Backcountry Publications, a Division
of Countrymen Press
PO Box 175, Woodstock VT 05091-0175
The popular "25 Rides in ...." series are
Backcountry publications. These are a
lot of fun and helpful for longer tours
as well as day trips.

Wilderness Press
2440 Bancroft Way, Berkeley CA 94704
The inventory here includes
interesting general how-to books

Ragged Mountain Press, a Division of
McGraw Hill
PO Box 220, Camden ME 04843
Ragged Mountain also has lots of
interesting outdoor recreation books.

Van der Plas Publications
1282 7th Avenue, San Francisco CA
94122
This is a source for bicycle-related
books, including this one.

Bicycle Organizations

Adventure Cycling Association
(formerly Bikecentennial)
50 East Pine St., PO Box 8308, Missoula
MT 59807-8308 Tel 800 755-2453,
membership@adv-cycling.org
http://www.adv-cycling.org.
        The yearly *Cyclists Yellow Pages*
is one of the most valuable resources
around for almost any aspect of biking
that you can think of. They sponsor
group tours, most notably across the
U.S. and publish excellent cycling

maps for many U.S. routes. You will find many tour operators listed as well. Their publication Cyclosource is a mail order catalog of selected gear and information. Members can take their bicycles by air for free by booking through their tour agency.

League of American Bicyclists
1612 K Street, NW, Suite 401,
Washington DC 20006 Tel 202
822-1333 bikeleague@bikeleague.org
http://www.bikeleague.org
   The strongest advocacy organization in the U.S., LAB publishes a yearly Almanac of Bicycling that is lists organizations for advocacy, education and recreation including tour operators. They sponsor large road rallies rather than tours, emphasizing community spirit and providing workshops on cycling skills. LAB actively promotes bicycling, bicycle education and laws and roadways that accommodate bicycles and cyclists. LAB has a "Bikes fly free" program as well with more options than Adventure Cycling.

Local Bicycle Clubs

They're everywhere, they're everywhere! Check your local telephone book and neighborhood bicycle shops as well as LAB's almanac. These groups provide incentive, companionship and lots of helpful advice.

Other Helpful Organizations

Hostelling International (American Youth Hostels, AYH)
National Administration Office 733

15th St. NW Suite 840 Washington DC 20005 Tel 202 783 6161
Hiayhserv@hiayh.org
http://www.hiayh.org

U.S. Parks National Net
http://www.us-national-parks.net/index.html

World National Parks
http://www.world-national-parks.net

The Great Outdoors
http://www.the-great-outdoors.net

Interesting Web sites

The Bicycle Web
http://www.bicycleweb.com

Bicyclopedia
http://homepage.interaccess.com/~opcc/bc/ "A comprehensive encyclopedia of bicycles and bicycling by U.S. Bicycle Corporation." Actually, more of a dictionary and glossary but helpful.

Pete's BikIndex by Pete Ruchelshaus
http://www.bikindex.com

Sheldon Brown's Web Site
http://sheldonbrown.com/bicycle_links.html

Map Sources

Adventure Cycling Association
150 East Pine St. PO Box 8308,
Missoula MT 59807-8308 Tel 800
755-2453,
membership@adv-cycling.org
http://www.adv-cycling.org.

DeLorme
Two DeLorme Drive, PO Box 298
Yarmouth ME 04096 Tel 207 846 8900
Fax 207 846 7051 Info@delorme.com
http://www.delorme.com De Lorme
also has an interactive CD/ROM
called Topo USA. I use this frequently

En-Route Maps, Inc.
1947 North Lindsay Road, Suite 106,
Mesa AZ 85213 Tel 602-641-7276 Fax
800-619-MAPS
http://www.en-route.com

International Map Trade Association
(IMTA)
Linda Mickle, Conference Coordinator,
PO Box 1789, Kankakee IL 60901
Tel 815-999-4627 Fax 815-999-8320
imta@maptrade.org
http://http://www.maptrade.org

Maps by Mail
PO Box 52, San Leandro CA 94577 Tel
510-483-8911

Maps WorldWide
PO Box 1555 Melksham SN126XJ UK
Tel 4401225707004 Fax 44 0 8700
558646
Customers@mapsworldwide.co.uk
http://www.mapsworldwide.co.uk

Michelin Travel Publications
PO Box 3305, Spartanburg SC
29304-3305 Tel 800-223-0987 or
800-423-0485

Rand McNally Map and Travel Stores
150 South Wacker Drive Chicago IL
60606 Tel 800 234 0679 Fax 312 443
9540 http://randmcnallystore.com

United States Geological Survey,
(USGS)
Information Services, Box 25286,

Denver, CO 80225 Tel 800-HELP-MAP
and 800-USA-MAPS Fax 303-202-4693
http://www.usgu.gov/USGS

On-line Booksellers

http://www.adventuroustraveler.com

http://www.amazon.com

http://www.globecorner.com

http://www.gorpbooks.com

http://www.countrymanpress.com

Bicycle Packs

Bicycle shops tend to have few choices
for packs so I suggest you look at some
of the mail order options before
making your decision

Bell Sports/ Blackburn
Route 136 East Rantoul IL 61866
Tel 800 456 2355
Fax 217 893 9054
desk@bellsport.com
http://www.bellsports.com

Bike Pro USA (also sells hard bicycle
cases)
3701 West Roanoke Phoenix AZ 85009
Tel. 800 338 758
silberman@uswest.net
http://www.bikeprousa.com

Cannondale
9 Brookside Place, Georgetown CT
06829
Tel 800 245 3872
E-mail cdale01@unterserv.com
http://www.cannondale.com

Jandd Mountaineering
30 S Salsipuedes St. Santa Barbara CA

93103
Tel 805 564 2044
http://www.jandd.com

Ortlieb USA
1402 20th Street NW Suite No. 7
Auburn WA 98001
Tel 253 833 3939 Fax 253 833 4559
OrtliebUSA@aol.com
http://member.aol.com/ortliebusa/or
tlieb.htm

Robert Beckman Designs
19350 Fairview Dr. Bend OR 97701
Tel 541 388 5146
http://www.coinet/~beckman

Serratus
Pelion Mountain Products
3103 Thunderbird Crescent , Burnaby
BC V5A3G1, Canada
Tel 604 444 3348
Fax 604 444 4011
Info@serratus.com
http://www.serratus.com

To make your own panniers, try:

Outdoor Patterns
2359 Ames Court, Laramie WY 82072
panniers@aol.com
http://members.aol.com/bikepan/pa
nnier.html/

Bicycle Manufacturers that Advertise a Model Designed for Touring

Factory Models

Cannondale
9 Brookside Place, Georgetown CT
06829

Tel 800 245 3872
E-mail cdale01@unterserv.com
http://www.cannondale.com

Fuji
118 Bauer Dr., PO Box 60 Oakland NJ
07436
Tel 800 631 8474
Fujibike@aol.com
http://www.fujibike.com

Green Gear Cycling
3364 W 11th Ave. Eugene OR
Tel 800 777 0258
info@bikefriday.com
http://www.bikefriday.com

REI
1700 45th St. E., Sumner WA 98352-000
Tel 800 426-4840
Services@mail.rei.com
http://www.rei.com

Rivendell Bicycle Works "Heron Tour"
1561 B Third Ave., Walnut Creek CA
94596
Tel 925 933 7304
Fax 925 933 7305
Rivbici@earthlink.com
http://rivendelbicycles.com

Softride Bicycles
4208 Meridian No. 2 Bellington WA
98227
Tel 800 557 6387
Fax 360 647 1884
http://www.softride.com

Terry Precision Cycling for Women
1704 Wayneport Road, Macedon NY
14502
Tel 800 289 8379
Fax 315 896 2104
Talktous@terrybicycles.com
http://www.terrybicycles.com

Trek
801 W Madison Waterloo WI 53594
Tel 800 369 8735
Fax 414 478 2774
http://www.trekbikes.com

Custom Designs

Bilenky Cycle Works
5319 N 2nd St. Philadelphia PA 19120
Tel 800 213 6388
Fax 215 329 5380
Artistry@bilenky.com
http://www.bilenky.com

Bruce Gordon Bicycles
613 2nd St. Petaluma CA 94952
Tel and Fax 707 762 5601
http://www.bgcycles.com

Co Motion also has bicycle travel cases
222 Polk St. Eugene OR 97402
Tel 541 342 4583
Fax 541 342 2210
comotion@teleport.com
http://www.teleport.com/~comotion

Croll Cycles
718 Washington Ave. N Suite 404
Minneapolis MN 5540
Tel 800 944 2453
Fax 612 334 5656

Davidson Handbuilt Bicycles
2116 Western Ave. Seattle WA 98121
Tel 800 292 5374
Fax 206 441 1815
Feedback@davidsonbicycles.com
http://www.davidsonbicycles.com

Rivendell Bicycle Works
1561 B Third Ave., Walnut Creek CA
94596
Tel 925 933 7304
Fax 925 933 7305

Rivbici@earthlink.com
rivendelbicycles.com

Waterford Precision Cycles
816 W Bakke Ave. Waterford WI 53185
Tel 414 534 4190
Fax 414 534 4194
wpc@waterfordbikes.com
http://www.waterfordbikes.com

Bicycle Travel Cases

The Bike Box
1729 E. Commercial Blvd. Suite 290 Ft
Lauderdale FL 33334
Tel 800 900 1663
http://bikebox.com

The Bike Pak
Tel 800 7587257

Bike Pro USA
3701 West Roanoke Phoenix AZ 85009
Tel. 800 338 758
silberman@uswest.net
http://www.bikeprousa.com

Co Motion
222 Polk St. Eugene OR 97402
Tel 541 342 4583
Fax 541 342 2210
comotion@teleport.com
http://www.teleport.com/~comotion

Crate Works
Box 125 Silver Lake NH 03875
Tel 800 934 5214
http://www.crateworks.com

Gorillium Systems
Tel 800687 7225
http://www.greerinc.com

Pedal Pack
Box 788 Porterville CA 93258
Tel 888 733 3520

Performance Bicycle Shop
PO Box 2741, Chapel Hill NC 27514
Tel 800 727-2433
Fax 800 727 3291
http://www.performancebike.com

Trico Sports Iron Case
Tel 800473 7705

Trailers and Other Options for Kids and Gear

Adams Trail-a-bike
Purchase through
Mud, Sweat and Gears
5340 NW Cache Road Lawton OK
73505
Tel 580 355 1808
Fax 580 355 1884

Baby Jogger Trailer
2609 River Road Yakima WA 98902
Tel 800241 1848

The Bike Trailer
BicycleR Evolution 985 Irving Road
Eugene OR 97404
Tel 800 357 2773
Bsi@rio.com
http://www.rio.com

Burley Trailers
Burley Design Cooperative, 4020
Stewart Road, Eugene OR 97402
Tel 800 311 5294
Fax 541 687 0436
http://www.burley.com

Bob Trailers
Bob Inc., 3641 Sacramento Drive No. 3,
San Luis Obispo CA 93401

Tel 800 893 2447
Fax 805 543 8464
Bob@bobtrailers.com
http://www.bobtrailers.com

The Caboos
Cycle Components PO Box 3480 La
Habra CA 90632
Tel 800 247 9754

CycleTote
517 North Link Lane Fort Collins CO
80524
Tel 800 747 2407
Cycletote@cycletote.com
http://cycletote.com

Green Gear Cycling
3364 W. 11th Ave. Eugene OR 97402
Tel 800 777 0258
Fax 888 394 7797
Info@bikefriday.com
http://www.bikefriday.com

The Tandem Link
93 Freedom Road Sewell NJ 08080
Tel 888 274 3327
http://www.tandem-link.com

Schwinn Joyrider Trailer
Tel 800 724 9466
http://www.schwinn.com

Traveling Tikes sells many different
kinds of trailers and
hitches
PO Box 491534 Los Angeles CA 90049
Tel 877 698 4537
Fax 310 470 8274
http://www.travelingtikes.com

Bicycle Manufacturers that Advertise a Model Designed for Women

Bianchi
21371 Cabot Blvd., Hayward CA 94545
Tel 510 264 1001
Fax 510 264 2099

Cannondale
9 Brookside Place, Georgetown CT
06829
Tel 800 245 3872
E-mail cdale01@unterserv.com
http://www.cannondale.com

Fat City Cycles
Tel 802 888 8800
Yobetty@aol.com
http://www.fatcitycycles.com

Marinoni USA
PO Box 335, Pittsford VT 05763-0335
Tel and Fax 802 483 6743
Marinoni@sover.net
http://ourworld.compuserve.com/ho
mepages/Fbeauchemin/

Performance Bicycle Shop
PO Box 2741, Chapel Hill NC 27514
Tel 800 727-2433
Fax 800 727 3291
http://www.performancebike.com

Rivendell Bicycle Works
1561 B Third Ave., Walnut Creek CA
94596
Tel 925 933 7304
Fax 925 933 7305
Rivbici@earthlink.com
http://rivendelbicycles.com

Rodrigues Bicycles
Tel 206 527 1384
Fax 206 527 8931
http://www.rodcycle.com

Terry Precision Cycling for Women
1704 Wayneport Road, Macedon, NY
14502
Tel 800 289 8379
Fax 315 896 2104
Talktous@terrybicycles.com
http://www.terrybicycles.com

Trek
801 W Madison Waterloo WI 53594
Tel 800 369 8735
Fax 414 478 2774
http://www.trekbikes.com

Waterford Precision Cycles
816 W Bakke Ave. Waterford WI 53185
Tel 414 534 4190
Fax 414 534 4194
wpc@waterfordbikes.com
http://www.waterfordbikes.com

Vendors with Either Mail Order Catalogs or Nationwide Stores

Agee Bikes
7439 W. Broad Street, Richmond VA
23294
Tel 804 672 8614
Fax 804 756 0468
Info@ageebike.com
http://www.ageebike.com

Bike Nashbar
Mail order catalog only. Some good
gear and prices, but again, not
specifically for touring
4111Simon Rd. Youngstown OH 44512
800-627-4227 or 800 774 5348
mail@nashbar.com
http://www.nashbar.com

Campmor
Inexpensive camping gear by mail or
from their huge warehouse in New
Jersey.

PO Box 700-8B, Saddle River NJ
07458-0700
Tel 800 525 4784
Customer-service@campmor.com
http://www.campmor.com

Eastern Mountain Sports (EMS)
327 Jaffrey Road, Petersborough NH
03458
Tel 888 463 6367
Customerservice@emsonline.com
http://www.shopems.com

Performance Bicycle
There are Performance Bicycle shops
although there seems to be a trend
toward becoming a mail order catalog
business only. While there is little
available specifically for touring,
Performance catalogs have many
goodies
PO Box 2741, Chapel Hill NC 27514
Tel 800-727-2433
www.performance.com

Recreational Equipment, Inc., (REI)
Co-operative with a one-time fee of
US$ 15. They sell gear for many sports
and have their own line of bicycles

including an inexpensive touring
bicycle. They sponsor tours, some of
which are by bicycle only or a
combination of biking and another
sport, such as walking, canoeing, etc.
1700 45th St. E., Sumner, WA
98352-000
Tel 800 426-4840
Services@mail.rei.com
http://www.rei.com REI

TOP, The Outdoor Professional
Lots of general merchandise for
outdoor recreation
666 Odana Road No. 135, Madison WI
53719
Tel 608 236 0470
Info@theoutdoorprofessional.com
http://www.theoutdoorprofessional.c
om

Velotique
1592 Queen Street East Toronto
Ontario Canada M4L1G1
Tel orders 800 363 3171
Tel information 416 466 3171
Fax 416 465 8156
Info@velotique.com
http://www.velotique.com

Bibliography

Books on Bicycle Touring

Richard A. Lovett. *The Essential Touring Cyclist*. Ragged Mountain Press, 1994. After the book you are now reading, this is the next best. Don't be put off by all the technical stuff on repairs, etc.

Rob Van der Plas. *The Bicycle Touring Manual*. Bicycle Books, 1993. There is much in this book that is good, especially technical information.

Steve Butterman. *Bicycle Touring: How to Prepare for Long Rides*. Wilderness Press, 1994. This short book has the right attitude, although it is a bit sparse on details.

Books on Bicycle Repair and Maintenance

Tom Cuthbertson and Rick Morrall. *The Bike Bag Book*. Berkeley, CA: Ten Speed Press, 1981. An excellent book to carry with you on tour if you do not feel confident to handle any situation. Most likely you will not need it, but if you do run into problems, this book will save your sanity and your tour.

Tom Cuthbertson. *Anybody's Bike Book*. Berkeley: Ten Speed Press. In my opinion, this is the best book for a novice to buy for bike repair and maintenance.

Rob Van der Plas. *The Bicycle Repair Book: The New Complete Manual of Bicycle Care*. Bicycle Books, 1993.

Richard Ballantine and Richard Grant. *Richard's Bicycle Repair Manual*, DK Publishers Merchandise, 1994.

Index

Other Cycling Resources Books from Van der Plas Publications

Cycling Across North America
Lue and Shannon Christian
272 pages with maps and photographs
U.S. list price $16.95 (ISBN 1-892495-24-4)

Cycling clear across the North American continent is one of the greatest challenges in cycletouring. The authors give you clear directions and background information for a relatively relaxing route.

Cycling the Rhine Route
John Powell
282 pages with maps and photographs
U.S. list price $16.95 (ISBN 1-892495-23-6)

For over a thousand years, the Rhine river has been the major route linking Western Europe's diverse cultures. The author shows you an easy route to follow and gives all the interesting background information.

Buying a Bike:
How to Get the Best Bike for Your Money
Rob van der Plas
96 pages
U.S. list price $9.95 (ISBN 1-892495-17-1)

Time for a new bike or accessories? This book shows how to select them so they match your needs, whether for sport, recreation, commuting, or touring.

A Woman's Guide to Bikes and Biking
Julie Harrell
96 pages
U.S. list price $9.95 (ISBN 1-892495-11-2)

Women's needs are different, and in this book, Julie Harrell shows you how to select the best gear and how to get the most out of your bike.